HORSE

ON FIRE

Published by Evelyn May at Amazon

Cover art by Evelyn May.

CHAPTER ONE

Green with Neglect

Our story began with suffering. It started with the ache in my heart that came from seeing the starving Arabian mare and the anger I had about how life and ignorance could create such a situation. It began with the agony of existence the poor mare had gone through for the past year, beginning with when a horse that had been somewhat cared for was given to someone completely ignorant of the amount of care, specialized knowledge and financial resources required to tend to horses properly.

I've described in "Round Pen, Square Horse" how I met Valhalla. Although I admire most horses I see, or at least find some quality that is aesthetically pleasing to me, this mare was an exception. Her half starved state made her head look large and knobby, she had a large warty growth on one ear, and a deformed nose with missing hair. Her tucked up abdomen made her look more like a rangy greyhound than an aristocratic Arab. Big chunks had been cut out of her scraggly mane and tail.

Yet from the moment I saw Valhalla, a battle started raging inside of me. Unfortunately, I'd come across many other horses in my life that were in sorry shape. Being involved in the horse world means you are sometimes exposed to the dark side. Although horses are large and expensive to keep, it can be fairly easy for an ignorant person to buy a horse and get in over their head. Even worse, there are those who know what horses need and consciously don't provide it for them. Selfish people prioritize their time and convenience over the care of an animal dependent on them. I've seen those with horses in daily pain that won't spend fifty cents a day for pain medication, but show up at the barn to look at that horse each day while holding their three dollar cup of coffee.

People keep horses in stalls that are rarely cleaned and don't let them out for weeks and months at a time. People forget to provide water for horses, don't provide necessary vet care, or let their hooves grow until they are so long they curl up like elf shoes. I'd seen these things many times over the years, and learned that it is impossible to save every horse and the most I could usually do was provide some education, a little financial assistance, or help find a new home for an unwanted horse.

Despite these experiences, despite the fact that I was practiced at turning away and willing myself to stop feeling deeply about things I had no control over, when I saw Valhalla something triggered inside of me. This horse was different.

Knowing I had another horse that took my time, money and attention, believing I could help tremendously with getting Valhalla healthy and able to be ridden, part of me was convinced that after several months I'd be able to help this mare find a new and wonderful home. That was a small part. All the rest of me, including the deepest and most soulful parts, wanted to keep Valhalla desperately. For some reason, what mattered to me most was absolutely guaranteeing that this horse would never have to suffer from neglect again. The only way I knew that could happen for certain was if I owned her for the rest of her life.

My conscience fought me. It felt like drowning, as if doing the thing I was supposed to do would pull me under and giving in to what my heart wanted would save me. Since I'm not a weak person, I fought hard. If there was not also good in what I wanted, in saving Valhalla and keeping her forever despite the fact that I was not supposed to have a second horse, that it might cause problems with my marriage, and perhaps my finances, and that I might not have the time to give this horse all that she deserved, I know I would have been strong enough to follow my conscience. As it was, I gave in and swam toward her light.

From the beginning, I loved her helplessly. It was unavoidable. She was ugly and sad, so I loved her from pity. Soon she began to transform and I loved her fighting spirit. Eventually she turned into a beautiful, powerful, exuberant horse with two full measures of spirit flowing out of her. That was when I began to love her the most.

Valhalla came to me as "Sophie," but my friends said that name sounded like a sad story, and I wanted her to have a happy one. So she became Valhalla, in my mind a synonym for the heaven I wanted her to experience with me and under my care.

Getting to know a horse that has only had negative experiences with people can be difficult. People talk about gaining a horse's trust and respect. I like to think of it as forming a friendship. In order to be friends, you have to get to know one another. That can be trickier if there is already a wall of mistrust built up.

Halla at first viewed me with suspicion. Yet, as with many Arabians, she didn't fight hard to protect herself but only stayed always ready to get away. When you had her in a small area, she knew she was trapped and would stand as you approached. She appeared always ready to defend herself, but would wait and not be aggressive, I assume waiting for the first strike. Thankfully, many horses are like this or so many would be terribly dangerous, after having dealt with abuse.

In the open, she would run and run, never allowing a person to get close. It was an interminably slow process to adapt her to allowing a person to approach, put a halter on and lead her away. It took time, patience, reconditioning and avoiding triggers that reminded her of tricks and painful things that had been tried on her in the past. The dent on her nose spoke of some unfortunate event or mishap with being haltered or tied.

As we got to know each other, there was a lot of time just spent in each other's company. Usually I had another horse with us, so Halla could see that the other horse was not afraid and happy to be around me. There was a lot of skin care, hoof care, health care, handling and grooming. This helped Halla learn that everything at her new home only made her feel good and healthier.

Along with teaching Halla that handling from humans would always be positive now and that only good things would be happening to her, she needed a general education. For starters, she needed to learn to lead politely, to stand tied, to wear a bridle and saddle, and to lunge. Since we didn't know if any of these things had been taught to her, or if they had been taught poorly, it was best to start over at the beginning.

Halla's former owner had signed her over to me, after some persuasion. She "loved" the two neglected horses we'd rescued from her after bringing them in for training at her request. It was a surprise to her to hear that they were in sorry shape, with Halla's friend Jack the Thoroughbred a week or two away from starving to death. The best incentive for the owner to let go was financial. After hearing how much it would cost to get the horses healthy, she was willing to let them go.

The owner said that Jack was a former racehorse, and Valhalla had been through a thirty-day training program when young. Now at thirteen, Halla was more than rusty on whatever those thirty days had entailed. However, she remembered the saddle and bridle, and had the basics of leading and standing tied. She did not know anything about being lunged.

It's always interesting teaching a horse to lunge. I'm not one to do a lot of lunging, or to be very particular about having the horse go around in a very formal manner. Yet it is important to me that horses know how to lunge. For one thing, it's a great way to introduce the words "walk," "trot," "canter," and "whoa." This is very helpful when you start riding, because the horse already associates the word with a particular gait. So it is an additional reinforcement to help them learn what you mean by certain bit, seat and leg cues.

There is a balance with the confused horse on a line, teaching them to move forward by applying a little driving pressure, but keeping them also from either turning and heading away from the handler, or turning in too close to the handler. Usually I err on the side of turning them in rather than driving the horse away, at first. So it appears to be a drunken weave with the horse getting pulled in, then pushed back out on the circle, then taking a few steps and coming in again. Eventually the concept of going around the handler is figured out. It all falls apart as each new gait is introduced, but eventually the horse is going around in a circle smoothly. Halla was no exception.

Our first several rides were in the small, outdoor arena at the boarding stable. Halla had the problem that many green horses have of getting "stuck." A horse's first thought is not to go around and around the perimeter of an open space. You get the horse to walk forward and then turn back the way you just came from, and then turn back again, and the horse starts to say "Wait a minute, are you just messing with me?"

It's far easier to teach a horse directional movement if you are doing something a horse understands. Such as walking around a small hill, or avoiding a tree. But it feels safer to begin with a horse inside a fenced area with good footing, such as an arena. The one thing you need to know is if a horse understands "stop." Equally important is that the horse understands how to turn well, because equine brakes have been known to get sticky when certain circumstances arise – it's like being in a car and hydroplaning through deep water. Suddenly you're pushing down hard on the brake pedal and nothing is happening.

As I was attempting to teach Halla about turning and stopping inside the arena, she was having some issues with my unreasonable ideas of going up and down a small and boring space for no reason. Every now and again she'd plant her front feet, kick a hind leg up and out to the side, and swish her tail dramatically. I'd listen to the protest and get her unstuck by going in a different direction. Then she'd figure out that even though we were going another way, we were still following these meaningless, inane patterns. Once that thought crossed her mind, she'd lash out again.

It seemed as though bringing another experienced horse into the arena might help Valhalla see that this was something horses did, even if she didn't understand it. We followed the other horse for a few minutes before Halla figured out that the horse was a complete idiot, wandering in meaningless circles. Then she refused to follow him.

Well, I was satisfied that we had at least a little directional steering and some stop and go, so before I ended up with a disdainful horse we stopped the arena work and went out on the trails.

CHAPTER TWO

Uneasy

Our first ride was heavenly. My friends Dawn and Lynn owned the small, private boarding stable where I kept Halla and my other mare, Amore. Our other good friend, Shania came out with us on the first ride, which we planned to keep very short.

Halla had quickly gained weight and her hooves were in good condition, but Jack, the Thoroughbred rescued along with her still had serious hoof cracks and had not built up any real muscle yet. He also had the worst case of scratches on all four legs I had ever seen. We were not taking him out for exercise yet, not wanting him to lose any of the hard-earned weight we'd put on him in the past couple of months.

The horses we chose to take out were Beau, Booker, Raja, Bibi and Scout, all good role models for a very green horse's first trail ride except for Bibi, who was still young and green but coming along. Two of the teens that regularly took riding lessons from Lynn were riding along.

We went up the road, and down a short trail that led by a farmhouse. The trail was a short length of gravel road that tapered off into grass, and dead-ended at the edge of a dense wood. It seemed like a good place to trot the horses, and since everything felt good I told the others to try a canter. We cantered the last two hundred yards or so before the woods, and Halla's canter was smooth and lovely. I was quite pleased, and commented on how nice her canter was, rocking and well cadenced. It seemed to me that this horse was going to easily shape into a great riding horse.

With the dense barrier of underbrush before us, all the horses stopped easily and naturally. That was not the first or the last time I've thought a horse was going to be easy to work with, only to find out there is more to the story. I'm not sure what happened that day, perhaps the newness of the situation had Halla squeezing her abdominal muscles tightly and flattening her gait. Perhaps she was still weak from being starved, and was dragging along. All I know is that there was never another ride where I experienced such a smooth and lovely canter from her. She was about to come into her own, and this horse did not have anything easy or smooth about her. She was all about explosive power rather than easy riding gaits.

6

When I bought Amore, she was unhandled and shy, so it took awhile to get her used to having my hands all over her body and touching her ears, legs and underbelly. Halla was also unused to being touched. She'd been apparently either ignored or manhandled for most of the years she'd spent after her brief period of training in her youth. Since she had rain rot everywhere and the sarcoid on her ear needed treatment, she soon grew used to me touching her ears, head and body.

Even though I'd provided pleasant grooming sessions and scratches to favorite spots for many years, Amore always remained ungrateful. She'd once in awhile rub her head into the brush, or appreciate a good udder cleaning, but mainly she seemed to simply feel it was her due as an aristocratic Arabian to have her staff massage her daily.

Halla was different. After only about a week of handling, she became very appreciative of the daily grooming she'd gone without for so many years. I'd set down her bucket of pelleted feed that most horses go crazy over and she'd leave it and come over to stand quietly with her eyes closed while getting brushed. She'd lean into the grooming or put her head down, and obviously enjoyed how it made her feel.

That being said, she did reserve some rights to privacy. The first time I lifted her tail and swiped some hanging piece of dirt off her hindquarters, she immediately double barreled the wall behind her with both hind legs. Thankfully I had been standing to the side, following basic horse safety measures.

Also, she never did adapt to having her udder touched. We worked on this for quite a few months before I gave in to her rules. The rules were: you could swipe once, fast with your hand to knock off some dirt. She'd simply tense up her back and swish her tail. She'd allow a second swipe if you missed something, and that would generate a squeal and lifting one hind leg in warning. If you ever tried a third swipe, or tried to get in deeper to wipe something off, the hind legs would start flying. No amount of reprimanding would ever curtail this behavior. However, she would let me rinse her udder off with a hose if it got too dirty. Apparently, a hand underneath the belly felt too much like a naughty foal trying to nurse off someone other than his mother. That deserved a kick.

It was not difficult to teach Halla the basics of being ridden. Since I preferred to ride in an English saddle, it was what I used on her, along with a simple D ring snaffle bridle. She was a quick study, and easily learned to respond well to cues. It wasn't long, however, before her competitive nature revealed itself.

Halla was not one to go along happily at the back of the herd or allow other horses to pass her. Since I wanted to teach her that she needed to both lead and follow other horses on rides, I made her take various positions as we went out riding with other horses.

She wanted desperately to always be in front. Cheyenne, the extremely hot Appendix bred ex-racehorse that Lynn usually rode also was a front horse. However, Cheyenne was a natural leader, a horse that others respected and deferred to. Halla was usually content to take the second place on rides when Cheyenne went along, but still would try to fight her way up to second place; if Cheyenne was left at home, she would want to be in front of the other horses.

On some occasions Cheyenne would be in a more passive mood and allow horses to ride up next to her or even a little in front. If Lynn said Cheyenne was not going to be passed on a certain day, we all listened and made sure our horses did not challenge her. We all knew that if Cheyenne got too worked up, she was bound to lose control and start running. As the natural leader, if Cheyenne began running, most likely the other horses would follow. That would seem like a competition to Cheyenne, and it was always unpredictable how long it would take all the horses to slow down.

Usually Cheyenne took care of the problem herself. On the two-lane logging roads, if a horse got too close to her and she didn't want them to pass, she'd often drift over in front of the other horse and block their progress. On a narrow trail, she'd turn diagonally and effectively leave no room for the other horse to travel past her. Even on a wide road, at a full run, sometimes when she didn't feel like just running off and leaving the other horse in the dust, Cheyenne would instead cut the other horse off so they couldn't go faster than the speed she wished to go.

Each of us controlled our individual horses, except somehow they all were controlled by Cheyenne more than by each rider. Cheyenne was herself a horse that had been discarded and would have never found a place in life if it weren't for Lynn. As with many horses that have dangerous issues, she was never going to become as simple to manage as a mellow horse that had never learned that a human's control was finite. In the beginning, Cheyenne would bolt through a double bridle at times, yet Lynn gained the horse's cooperation and eventually was able to manage her very well almost all of the time. She even downgraded her to riding in just a Kimberwicke, which affords little leverage. But with a horse like Cheyenne there was always careful compromise, and you could not for example ever ask her to hold steady while another horse went galloping away in front of her.

When side by side with other horses, Cheyenne had some kind of hypnotic power. Even the least competitive, unmotivated or lazy horse would get eye to eye with Cheyenne and suddenly feel the need to race. Something about her large, black, almond-shaped eye would wake the horse right up and have him trying to match her stride for stride. Since Cheyenne was undeniably the fastest horse in any group, this was a challenge no horse could ever win. Probably most of them knew this, since they spent time in the fields together, but yet they always tried.

Eventually she'd tire of the game and in a moment, leave the other horse behind. The gap would continue to open between the horses until it was time for the run to end. If we were on curving trails, Cheyenne would soon be out of sight. Even on flat miles of beach, she'd soon be a tiny spec in the distance, and at least once she and her rider careened off the beach without the rest of us knowing because she was so far away.

Although Halla wished to be in front of a group of horses, she was as yet inexperienced on trails. She seemed to have a desire to be bold, but was uncertain about which things were dangerous and should be avoided. This meant our first rides were a strange mixture of Halla going strongly and courageously forward, and then cringing and cowering away from an unexpected sight. Even when Halla was spooking, she would attempt to appear as if she was not. She would veer suddenly away to the far side of the track we were trotting or cantering along, but while still trying to keep her speed up. It seemed like she had one eye on the other horses to not let them pass, and also to see if they were reacting to any object.

9

Often at first what threw her the most were patches of light or shadow. If she ran into a patch of light, she would sometimes just stop completely as if she'd hit a solid object. When filtered light pattered onto her head, she'd flinch like the rays were rocks raining down on her.

When she saw something concerning, her head would tilt, and she'd canter with one eyeball focused on the scary object, giving it space but trying to move boldly past it. All of that would be fine unless the object moved or she suddenly judged that it might be harmful. In those cases, she would suddenly leap to the side or stop.

When Halla stopped, she would stop dead. I've been on a couple of horses trained to do reining stops, and those could throw you forward if you weren't ready for it. But Halla would stop and instead of continuing to move forward for a step or two, at least with the front legs, she would just stop and her hind end would drop under. Not knowing this was about to happen, it would be impossible for me to stop my own momentum. Instead, I'd continue forward until my stirrups stopped me, or else my body slamming against Halla's shoulders and neck. At least a couple of times, I felt her ear tickling inside one of my nostrils. That was how close I was to riding right over the top of her neck.

It wasn't long before I realized I needed more than a simple snaffle to contain Halla. She was extremely smart and motivated about trying to go fast. When she had open road in front of her, she wanted to get moving. Even if there was no open road and only a horse's hind end in front of her on a narrow trail, she thought somehow she could just put her head up and push through or over the top of the other horse to get to the front. That was something I could not allow, having experienced in the past how horses often resent another horse running into their backside, and learned how easily a person can break a leg from those defensive kicks.

CHAPTER THREE

Tricks and Fixes

By now, I'd taught Halla the basics of riding. She knew how to turn, using her body, how to move away from my leg pressure, how to push forward and balance into a stop. We'd practiced standing still and stopping on a trail, staying in place while a rider mounted, and making large and small circles in both directions. She responded well to cues for slowing down when not feeling competitive. The issue was when we were behind another horse, trying to catch up or if Halla felt we were competing with another. At those times, she would just push through the snaffle, and even though I could sometimes control her speed by bending her through the body, or making her change leads, she would often get her way.

Halla tried to find tricks to use to go faster. One thing she tried was stretching her nose out as far as she could, then suddenly drawing it in as she took off. That way I'd have to pull the reins up quickly in order to make contact with the bit to slow her down, and she'd already be off running. Another trick she taught herself was to transition into a canter without changing anything in her body posture or stride. She'd be trotting and then immediately be cantering, and I wouldn't even feel her hind leg stretching to pick it up before she was in stride.

Something I had no idea about how to address was the fact that Halla's saddle – any saddle – would shift over to the left during a ride. At first I wondered if perhaps one of my legs was shorter than the other, and I'd never noticed, or if I was pulling the saddle off to the side as I mounted, and getting it unbalanced. However, this happened regardless of who rode her. At the time, we thought perhaps she moved crooked and this created the problem. In order to fix it, I would often ride with the left stirrup one hole shorter so it was weighted less. This helped the saddle stay upright.

Eventually I learned that some horses with front hooves that are uneven heights end up developing one shoulder muscle a lot more. Since Halla had large shoulders, the muscle behind the shoulder on the right side was larger, which meant the saddle would tend to get shifted to the left. That front hoof was wider and flatter, sitting lower to the ground. This meant that shoulder was weighted more and developed more over time.

The fix, which I didn't figure out for some years, was to work on getting the hooves so they weren't so unbalanced, to do a lot of work on developing the smaller shoulder, stretching out the bigger shoulder, and to ride in a treeless saddle for awhile to keep the saddle unaffected by the uneven muscles. This helped Halla become even enough to be ridden in a regular saddle with symmetrical panels. Prior to this, I added a shim to fill in the space around the smaller shoulder, which also helped a little but did not completely fix the problem.

Meanwhile, my crooked horse felt stiffer turning to the left and was outsmarting me when she wanted to take off. After a lot of reading, I decided to try a Kimberwicke bit on her. I found a single jointed, simple Kimberwicke, and she immediately responded better to it than a regular D ring snaffle. The chain was set so I had to pull back significantly in order to engage it, so as long as she was following my directions well she could choose to not have any real correction. But when she decided to see what she could get away with, I could engage the chain and it worked really well to get her head up if she tried to push down and forward, to pull her off stride when she was being really strong, and to hold her back when she was insisting on crawling over the top of another horse in her way.

In all of this, I never felt that my mare had any ill will toward me. She seemed to enjoy getting out and running around, seeing the various trails and competing with other horses. She wasn't challenging me, personally, but rather was fighting against the idea that she should control her speed or lose the race to other horses. All I felt was excitement, joy and a competitive spirit. She did not seem to have any angst toward me, although sometimes she would get so fired up that we would end up in a strategic battle. She would be fighting to run and let her energy out, I would be fighting to stay safe and control the speed.

We neither of us were directly fighting each other. It was a very rare occasion where my mare would stop listening, and instead we always seemed to be engaged in intense negotiations. We would negotiate each section of trail and how it should be managed - sometimes I'd give her a little extra say, while other times she'd give the nod to my idea. As I've heard a rider say about his horse, "We have an understanding." Over time, we worked out the details but it never was easy for me, and probably not for her either.

She'd have much preferred if a rider would just give her the freedom to do whatever she wished. On two occasions, I saw that happen, and it was pretty wild. Both times it was Lynn riding Halla, since Lynn was a fearless rider and was prone to letting a horse have a good run when they wanted to. The first time, we were riding on the beach and it seemed likely that Halla would stop when the other horses did. However, Lynn had let Halla go, and she was flying along feeling great, so she continued galloping until Lynn finally turned her sharply to one side and stymied her legs in a deep sand dune, where she was able to pull her up.

The second time, we were on a gravel logging road and Lynn didn't set Halla up for a gallop but instead just loosened the reins, leaned forward and let her go. Halla was surprised at the sudden freedom and burst into a gallop from nearly a standstill. She was wearing Renegade hoof boots on all her hooves, and that was only the second time I saw those boots come off. Halla scrabbled her legs in all directions, her mind taking off faster than her legs could follow. All four boots blew off in all directions, and Halla's legs were a blur as she took off up the hill. Fortunately, in that case the hill was very long and steep, so Halla was ready to be pulled up when Lynn reached the top. The rest of us came running up behind just a bit more slowly.

Halla quickly became very good at doing flying changes. It was something I inadvertently taught her, because I often had a lot of difficulty allowing her to burn off energy while still keeping her at the speed she needed to be at. She was not a horse you could trap or "shut down." I've heard that term used by riders, and it is a concept that only applies to horses that are not extremely hot blooded.

Some horses get excited or worked up, and can be calmed back down very quickly. They might try to run off after spooking, and the rider can do a one-rein stop and disengage the hind end, and after a minute or so the horse becomes calm. Perhaps if they are still excited you might direct their movement in a circle, or ask them firmly to stop and stand.

Others have a larger degree of excitability that can quickly turn into explosiveness if not managed properly. That is something a rider or handler cannot change, although a horse can adapt to an environment and daily work so it becomes less exciting for them.

Yet even that is relative. For example, Cheyenne could go on the same ride five days a week, and still have days where her mood was too explosive and if someone tried to keep her speed too slow (for example, make her walk instead of trot through a section), she would lose her mind and blow up. This presents in different ways with different horses, but is always dangerous and makes the horse less manageable in the long run. If the horse never feels trapped, their mind is more likely to stay with the rider. For those horses that lose their ability to think when overly excited, it is a very bad idea to put a lid on a boiling pot.

Some people might observe a horse behaving excitedly and think the owner has just not trained the horse properly or is even encouraging the behavior to show off. If the horse is merely inexperienced or over faced, the behavior will go away quickly and most horses cannot even be encouraged to act like that. From what I've seen, most often horses that are very hot have the excitedness innately, and it can only be managed and damped down a bit rather than trained away.

For those horses, trying to "shut them down" will often escalate their energy into explosive behaviors. If you try to force the horse to stand in one place or stay very slow, they will often boil over and do something like rear, start bucking, force through the aids and take off, or run sideways or backwards.

Since Halla had this type of energy, I had to find ways to keep her speed managed while still using up her excited energy in a harmless way. In the canter, I would have her bend and counter bend, which was difficult for her when I chose her stiffer side or had her bend contrary to the lead she was on. This would slow her down and keep her focused and not rushing away when other horses were cantering by. It was something that allowed me to practice having her behind the other horses and not racing at the canter.

However, she soon discovered that she could also burn off energy when very excited by throwing herself high in the air and changing her leads at the canter. Soon, when I asked her to stay slow and bend instead of rushing off, if she was too excited she'd do a flying lead change with every stride. Eventually I learned how to feel the balance and ride these, but at first I thought I'd get thrown off as she leaped and cavorted.

Often I would try to work on keeping Halla in a big, extended trot to help her burn off energy. She always preferred to canter, apparently believing that a trot was never going to lead to a gallop, while a canter was bound to eventually. I've read that horses can either be more efficient at a trot or a canter for endurance, based on their build and how they move. My belief is that Halla was more efficient at the canter, and had to work harder at the trot. Efficiency did not seem to be her primary objective in life, as she pranced and snorted and burned off energy excessively on every ride. Yet there was something about cantering that was easier or felt more right to her, so she spent most of her time trotting thinking about trying to break into a canter.

CHAPTER FOUR

Hoof In Boots

Other than me, those who rode Halla were only a select few. They had to be excellent riders and also be willing to go through the chess game negotiations through the entire ride. No one ever just went for a casual ride on Halla. She was always trying things to see what would happen. I always had to warn people that if we started trotting, Halla would be attempting to canter every thirty seconds or less, so if they wanted to stay trotting they would have to work very hard at it. Something else I would point out was that she was naturally crooked (before understanding about her large shoulder) and that it would take a lot of work to keep her moving down the trail straight.

On one ride up in the mountains, I was on a different horse and watching my friend Shania taking Halla down the trail. They weaved from side to side, and every few seconds Halla would catch Shania off guard and break into a canter. Knowing how difficult it was to prevent this behavior, I watched as Shania struggled, insisting she was having a nice ride, while Halla appeared to always be one chess move ahead on the board.

Valhalla was the horse that motivated me to learn hoof trimming. It was more like force than motivation, in the end. She was very tricky to trim at first, and when I was trying to adapt her to holding her hooves up for the farrier, she would rear up, pull her front hooves away and then slam them down. With her hind legs she was a bit snatchy, and would pump them toward you but never really tried to kick. That meant the first trim or two were very tricky, not the greatest job, and something I did with help from friends.

The logging roads we rode on were graveled and had large rocks in some areas. Since the horses were mostly all shod to deal with this rough footing, once Halla was going out on the trails we needed to get shoes on her. She was behaving much better, and I thought she would be fine for the farrier. However, when he showed up he took one look at her and asked if we could use ACE, a mild sedative injection.

Since we had some ACE on hand, I went ahead and gave Halla a shot. Still craning her head around and looking at everything brightly, after a time the farrier said we should try a second injection. When the second injection did nothing, the farrier suggested a third. This was something I was not comfortable with, not knowing what the safe dosage was. So the farrier left, but gave me a set of shoes in Halla's size. Dawn, Lynn and I set to work and after trimming Halla's hooves, nailed four shoes on her.

By this time, I'd learned basic trimming. Dawn and Lynn were proficient trimmers, having taken farrier classes. Dawn was strong enough to shape the shoes on their anvil, and we assisted each other with staying safe while holding Halla's legs up. The tricky part in my book is right after the nails are pounded through the hoof wall and the spiky end is sticking out at you. That's when the horse could move suddenly and slice you or herself open. But one of us was always there to quickly break off the nail end, and Halla did well enough for us, holding her hooves up for a minute or two which was long enough to get the shoes on.

Halla had sarcoids, which are similar to warts. She had a huge plaque-like one at the base of one inner ear, and several others on her legs and body. Behind each front pastern was another large, plaque-like area. I assumed these were also sarcoids. Within a day of shoeing Halla, I found out that those bumpy areas behind her front pasterns were actually scars. When she had shoes on, she would interfere at the faster gaits, stepping far enough forward with the hinds to clip herself. We tried adjusting her shoes and using protective boots, but in the end nothing worked. The shoes came off and my foray into using hoof boots for riding began.

17

At first we used Easyboots. They are black, made out of a rubber-like substance and can hold up to many miles of hard wear. The only issue we had was that they came off very frequently. All of this was part of my journey into learning about hoof trimming. Over time, I learned that the reason Halla interfered was because her toes were too long, which meant her hoof didn't break over soon enough for her to get out of her own way. Until I learned this, she often stepped forward at the gallop, caught the back of her Easyboots and either tore or flung them off into the bushes. Since Easyboots are black, we spent a lot of time looking in the bushes and down the roads for our missing boots. One problem I had was that the gaiters designed to help keep the Easyboots on the horses would rub Halla's scars behind her pasterns. I tried various wraps and socks but sometimes her scars would break open and bleed.

Lynn, Dawn and Shania used boots off and on, but found them very frustrating. Once we laughed very hard because Beau stepped out of a front boot, and then stepped into it with his hind hoof and began walking along wearing it on the back. The neighbors often took walks in the woods along the logging roads, and they would find our boots and set them on top of the gates so we could find them on later rides.

Eventually I moved away from the area and had to leave my good friends behind. This was a new phase in my life. Before moving down to this area of the coast, I'd only had my mare Amore, and had not been a very secure rider. Because of this, I'd ridden mainly in arenas and done only short trail rides out alone. After riding with Lynn, Dawn and Shania for a few years, training more horses and riding quite a few difficult ones, things were going to be very different. My plans were to take both Amore and Halla out on rides by themselves, at least until I found more people at my new barn to ride with.

It wasn't long before I discovered new boots called Renegades, and they were a game changer for me. To my surprise, when I tested them out they fit both my Arabs very well and stayed on their hooves much better than the Easyboots I'd used. I heard from some people that the newer Easyboots had better designs and stayed on horses better. That was something I didn't test out for myself, since I was able to put Renegades on all four hooves on both my horses, gallop around and go through mud, water, and rough terrain without losing boots. It took a long time to break my habit of looking down at each hoof periodically to see if the boots were on, but I soon found that I didn't need to. For Halla they were the perfect design because there was an opening in the back where the scars were on her pasterns, and we had no more issues with rubs.

Before I moved away from Lynn's barn, the four of us decided to do a twenty-five mile limited distance endurance ride. We always trained and rode the horses pretty hard, so only needed to add a little bit of mileage to get them ready for the ride. This was the second one we'd done, since Shania, Dawn and I had participated in one previously with Booker, Cassie and Amore. Those three horses were naturals and did very well.

The only problem was that the only other horse we thought would do well at endurance was Halla. Lynn was bigger than me and I thought if Amore was going to do such a long ride, she should have the lightest possible rider. By now she was twenty, in great shape, but still getting along in years. This would mean that Lynn would be on Halla instead of Amore. But for some reason whenever I thought of Lynn riding all those training miles on Halla, it made me feel jealous. This was strange, because I'd always liked people riding my horses, and thought it good for them.

What I started doing was talking about how maybe Amore was too old, and this deception made me feel guilty. It was difficult to decipher my own feelings. In the end, I confessed to my friends and Lynn was kind as always and understanding, and made no fuss about my silly selfishness. This is what led us to conditioning Maggie, the ex-broodmare Paint horse for endurance along with our three hot bloods. Poor Maggie.

The training went very well, and eventually you could barely recognize Maggie. She was as leaned out and light muscled as a stock horse can get, and although her mind was difficult to engage for all those miles she could physically do it. On the actual day of competition, Lynn had a difficult time for the last eight miles or so, keeping Maggie going at our pace. What made things more difficult was that Cassie and Booker were very calm and well behaved, but Halla was nutty.

Cassie was an extremely hot headed, big horse but she had this quirk in her nature that whenever she went to a new place she was calm and reliable. If you rode her several times in one place, she'd be super hot and frothy again. But that first ride she was always sweet and compliant.

Halla was the one driving the pace, and we made the mistake of taking off with all the other horses but in the middle of the pack. Which meant Halla thought we were either racing or else something was chasing this giant herd of horses, and from then on I used every muscle in my body to keep her from galloping away. Lynn often called out that Maggie was not going to be able to keep the pace, and I tried so hard to slow down. We thought about pulling Maggie back, but Lynn didn't think she'd finish on her own without the familiar herd. It was hard enough to motivate her as it was.

The horses all had good marks, in the end, and our training had been sufficient. We didn't mean to finish so far up in the race, but it was unavoidable. Holding Halla back for twenty-five miles was extremely punishing to my body. She did not have a mark on her, and did not seem sore the next day. Even Maggie seemed unfazed. In contrast, I remember standing on a three-inch tall step on my patio the day after the ride and summoning the courage to step down, knowing it was going to hurt quite a lot. That was when I realized some people do fifty and one hundred mile rides, and decided they must be some other breed of human. Our horses could do it, but could we? Something we haven't tried to figure out yet.

20

CHAPTER FIVE

Ditches and Dodges

Many very entertaining things happened while we were still at Lynn's barn. Once we went to the beach and were winding our way through some sandy trails on the dunes. Halla missed a turn, stepped off the trail and then she was standing in thick bushes that went almost up to her knees. She took a step forward, and the bushes tangled around her legs, causing her to trip and almost go down. She deposited me onto my back, where I lay flailing my limbs like an upside down turtle in the thick bushes. Meanwhile, she stepped back onto the trail and stood calmly waiting for her turtle to get free.

Halla and I sometimes went out alone from Lynn's barn, when everyone else was too busy to ride. One beautiful day I was out riding Halla along a grassy track that once was a logging road but had long since grown over. She was cantering along in one of the ruts, and I was letting the sun warm my face. I remember blinking slowly and when I opened my eyes, we were in the other rut on the other side of the road, still cantering lazily. I'd never felt the motion, but apparently during the blink when I'd had my eyes closed, Halla had spooked, and somehow leaped into the other lane without dislodging me.

As we progressed with Halla's training, I began working her over cavaletti and seeing if she had a natural ability to jump. Gradually, we worked over larger obstacles, starting with trot poles and then elevating them slightly. This worked very well, and soon she was trotting over very high jumps...the only problem was that as long as she could fit them under her belly at the trot, she wouldn't jump at all, just keep trotting. Even though it wasn't ideal, I had to put her toward very high jumps to get her to even make the effort. She didn't seem to care to jump at all, and on the trails would trot over big logs that the other horses were leaping.

Eventually over time, I worked on having her cantering over the jumps, but she usually wouldn't lift her canter either and would just let it come close to or even bang her belly. Strangely, when cantering and not jumping, she'd often leap high in the air and do her flying changes, but when "jumping," she would not elevate the canter at all. I guessed she was not meant to be a jumper, but she'd gladly plow over anything I pointed her at, without jumping.

One day I had the most spectacular dismount, when no one was around to see it. I was "jumping" Halla over some small jumps, which really meant we were cantering around an area with jumps in the pathway. We were in an indoor arena, and suddenly the big metal door pulled away from the building in the wind and banged loudly. Halla was landing her canter stride on the other side of the jump at that moment, and the second her front hooves hit the ground she popped them back up and leaped to one side. It was too fast for me to think, but my body reacted by stepping hard into the stirrup of the side we were leaping toward, and pushing my leg up and over the horse so I hopped up, flipped around and ended flying off the horse while spinning in a standing position, and landing nicely on the ground on my feet. I waited for the clapping but there was none.

Lynn, Shania, Dawn and I went to ride the beach trails on a sunny day, and Halla taught me about her generous nature. We hadn't been out to the trails for a while, and some of the Scotch Broom had grown quite a bit and taken over. Our timing was poor because the Scotch Broom was in full bloom, and we soon found ourselves squeezing through tight channels of yellow flowers. We were going down hills while sitting on our horses, but were unable to see the horse we were on. It was a trick to stay clamped onto the horse and not let the bushes push us off.

This was all a minor inconvenience for most of us, but Shania had allergies to the pollen and her nose soon began to swell and eyes run.

When we exited the end of the last trail, we looked around and saw that we and our horses were all coated in yellow powdery pollen. It was everywhere.

Now we were on a wide, flat, open trail and it went straight for as far as we could see. Dawn was leading so began to trot, and then canter. It was wide enough for any of us to pass if we needed to.

Since Dawn was on Cassie, she was traveling pretty fast on her large horse. Halla had eagerly leaped into the canter, and we cantered along for several minutes before Halla began ramping up her speed. I gave a little check on the reins, which was met by blankness. Suddenly there was no horse on the end of my reins. Halla was completely ignoring me. Just to make sure, I spoke through the reins again.

"Hello?" Nothing. I pulled hard, using a pulley rein type stop with one rein stabilized against her neck while the other cued intermittently, and began working on bending to get her back. No response.

Well, we had a ways to go, so I thought I'd give her some time to come back to me. We kept cantering, and Halla was stretching out at a good clip, blissfully. Cassie was still in front, but barely.

Periodically I'd try to talk to my horse, but she did not respond. Eventually, Cassie pulled up as the trail began to get twisty and Halla went shooting past her. After ignoring my cues for a bit longer, we came to a pretty good curve, which made Halla hesitate mentally, and I seized that moment to take over. She conceded, and slowed. The others soon caught up.

That was the day I realized that Halla knew she could take over a ride at any time. I believe many horses are fooled, and think the rider actually controls them, and that a bit is powerful enough to stop them. This works very well except for those rare occasions when a horse loses their mind, perhaps after getting stung by a hive of bees or something similar. Amore had been known to lose her mind on occasion. Halla was different. She was calmly thinking and not overly excited in this case, but yet understood clearly that she could take over and do whatever she wished.

I already understood that riding horses is only an illusion of control. We can never "control" an animal we are sitting on that weighs a thousand pounds, is not drugged and has all four feet on the ground. Obviously they can do whatever they want. However, many horses have been trained and taught to work with humans from a very young age, have never learned how little control humans actually have, or just go along with us due to conditioning and willing natures.

What I realized that day was how my lovely horse understood completely that I was not in control of her, yet on almost every occasion she would play the game with me and we would discuss her way and my way, and she would mostly concede. Even on the days when her will was strong, she'd still behave as though we were negotiating and discussing. Yet she knew all along that if she wished, she could just run on and on, ignoring me completely and there was nothing I could do about it.

Was this frightening? Actually, I found it quite beautiful. It showed me that a horse like Halla must enjoy our riding games or else she would refuse to participate. It made me believe that we did have a friendship, after all, and that something about me spoke to something in her that made her want to have a conversation on a day to day basis. It made me love and appreciate her even more, and all horses. How is it that horses are so powerful and physically apt, such independent thinkers with strong personalities, yet they let us have a part in everything they are?

CHAPTER SIX

Ethics and Adventures

Upon moving from the area, our first boarding barn stint was brief, and did not work out so well. At first, everything seemed ideal. We went back to a barn where I'd boarded before, and found a lovely house on the beach to rent that was only five minutes away. Soon we discovered the house was not safe to live in, and had to get out of the lease.

The barn had issues also. It sounded quite perfect, with the horses turned out almost all of the time, good hay, and a nice arena. The beach was so close; I thought I could ride to it.

One day I did take Amore across the highway to the beach, quite early in the morning to avoid traffic. Still, a semi drove by as I was leading her the eighth of a mile we had to be on the highway, the noise of his brakes startled her and her hooves skittered out on the gravel. Next thing I knew, she had fallen down and was lying flat on the side of the highway. She didn't seem injured when she got up, we made the trek to the beach, rode down a couple miles and visited the house we were renting. Although we made it back fine, it wasn't something I planned to repeat with either Amore or Halla.

Halla rapidly began to lose weight, and Amore was soon laid off riding due to getting a large hematoma on her hip from getting kicked. It turned out that the entire herd was getting fed off several square hay bales daily, and the aggressive horses were getting all the feed and fighting the others off. There were not enough feed stations for the dozen or so horses, so only about six of them got most of the hay. The barn owner was afraid of Halla, apparently because she was trying to lock her in a stall to eat her concentrated pellets while the other horses were still out, since I'd pointed out she was losing weight and my bags of grain were not getting more empty.

Halla had come to me with severe separation anxiety, and this treatment was bringing back the behavior. She also started getting more difficult to catch again, apparently because the other horses were spending a lot of time driving her around and away from the hay. According to the barn owner, Halla was lunging out over the stall door, not eating anything and then bursting out when she was finally released.

These things came to my attention slowly, and once I realized what was going on the horses were moved to a barn that was unfortunately a farther drive away.

During the couple of months we were at this barn, before moving the horses, I also discovered that things had changed for me since the last time I'd boarded there.

Now I liked to ride, really ride and go places. It turned out that the mile long jaunt down the road I'd previously enjoyed on Amore was far too short. Amore was out of commission, so I began taking Halla out to see if we could find places to ride. This proved very difficult.

The aerial maps I looked at online seemed to connect the road the barn was on with a lake. When I went down that road, there was a dead end and some large concrete blocks we had to snake through, and then we found ourselves in a large field. The field had a gravel trail around the edge, and I realized this had been a car racetrack I recalled hearing about when I was young. The raceway had been closed down for many years, and the county had purchased it to expand the walking trails that went around the lake.

Of course, the first thing I did was let Halla canter around the grassy field, which soon got a little dicey as we spooked at various things and I tried to stay slow enough to watch for holes. Next we went down the graveled walking path, which had some very frightening benches set up randomly along it. At the lake, I remembered a hiking path over a hill, which I set Halla on before realizing it was extremely narrow even for walkers, and the brushy trees were too low to pass under on a horse.

Holding my breath, we minced through while I smashed myself down onto Halla's neck, pushed the bushes aside as we squeezed through a couple tight gaps. At the end we went back the long way down the gravel roads, which I now saw were marked for pedestrians only. I tried to stay away after that, but without anywhere else to ride except an indoor arena or down a short road, I couldn't help sneaking back several more times in the late evenings.

Since we were not actually allowed to ride at the lake, I went down the road another direction and followed some gravel logging roads up into the hills to see if they went anywhere. Unfortunately, the only way to reach the longer roads was through private property, and the type of buildings on the property and secluded nature of it made it seem unwise to go and try to make myself acquainted. Skirting far around the edge of the property, I hoped my horse looked like a deer from far away, and also that the owner was not planning to shoot a deer for supper.

After all that, I found where the road was that met the mainline on the map, but discovered it had been seeded heavily by trees over the years of misuse and was now too overgrown to get through without heavy equipment.

There was one final place to try, and I found a trail through a sucking swamp that met up with a gravel road. This led far up into the hills, past a cell phone tower, and I was planning to explore it further when it became apparent the horses were not doing well and I needed to move them. By this time Halla was starting to look more ribby than was acceptable in my mind, and I did not want either horse to get kicked badly again.

Going down the road was never completely boring at this barn, because it was lined with cranberry bogs. The bogs were full of sprinkler systems that would randomly rear their heads all over the bogs and start spitting water. This sudden movement coming from multiple sources, along with the accompanied loud hissing was understandably quite startling for the horses at first. It wasn't long before Halla was nearly immune to the activity, however.

The new barn I moved the horses to was far out in the countryside. Our new rental house was an eleven mile drive away, at the edge of town, but it took about twenty minutes to drive out since the roads had many twisting curves. It was a beautiful drive with views of verdant fields and flowing rivers, enjoyable except for a couple days when it rained heavily and hundreds of frogs were hopping all over the road. Although it pained me, and I drove as slowly as I could, I'm sure I squished a few inadvertently.

The atmosphere at the new barn was quiet and peaceful. It had a daily routine, which the horses settled into and soon were healthy and at good weights again. Their daily turnout was with several other Arabs and young horses, so they enjoyed running around the large pastures. There was plenty of grass to eat and the horses were fed their hay inside stalls at night. The ghetto wars of the previous barn were soon forgotten.

As usual, my fellow boarders observed me and my horses. After a time, I got to know them well. One friend told me later that she would watch me tacking up Halla, and couldn't believe I was going to get on and try riding her. In a new setting, there was a lot of prancing going on through the tacking up process.

Unfortunately, during the first week at the new barn my timing was a bit off, and when I put the bit in Halla's mouth she swung her head wildly toward me and bashed me in the eye with the side of the Kimberwicke. This gave me a slight black eye, which was unfortunate since my coworkers at my new job did not know me very well yet. Thankfully, no one tried to give me any numbers for battered women hotlines or anything like that.

Even in a brand new setting, and feeling insecure, Halla always would settle the moment I landed in the saddle. Something about having the rider on board would calm her, since she knew we were now going to be heading out to work. Once someone was mounted, her expression would become serious and businesslike. Even if it came down to throwing the saddle on a moving target on her worst day, and struggling to keep hold of the girth while feeding the billets through the buckles, all of that would change when I got on her.

Halla had the greatest work ethic. You never had to tell her to go, or plead with her to pick up her speed or try harder. She always burned energy as if it were funneled up from the core of the planet into her hooves and was inexhaustible. What always amazed me was that I never saw her run out. For her, tired was only a theory, and one she did not subscribe to. I'm certain she felt tired sometimes, but she would never let on. She was truly a horse that would run herself into the ground if someone let her.

This was one of the reasons that Halla was my favorite horse to ride of all time. I'd saddle her up, get on, and she'd never think twice about heading out alone. She'd never waver or suggest that perhaps feeding time was nearly upon us, or act miffed because we just went out yesterday. I could tell she was often more eagerly interested in going out if we had other horses with us, but she'd still walk out with a peppy stride every single time, regardless.

How amazing it was to take out my horse, get on and ride anywhere I wanted, knowing my horse would be happy to take me there. Not only that, if I wanted to gallop on the trails, or trot for miles and miles, she'd be happy to oblige me.

That's not to say in a brand new environment Halla was steady as a rock and unflappable. First we tried the indoor and outdoor arenas, to acclimate ourselves a bit. Next, the barn owner pointed out that there was a trail through the woods that went up the hill behind her house. It was about a mile long, had some steep uphill and downhill sections, and both Halla and Amore did fine with it. Of course, Amore crept out at first, and I had to get off and lead her through some scary parts. Halla pretended that nothing about it scared her, while bobbling left and right as various light patterns hit us or we encountered crackling leaves or fallen logs.

CHAPTER SEVEN

Mountains

After several weeks, I finally asked the barn owner about the "endless miles" of logging road trails she'd mentioned when I'd first inquired about moving my horses to her facility. She brought her own horse out and led me up a trail that met with some gravel, and told me about another entrance to the logging roads I could use if I would ride half a mile down the main road.

Halla and I ventured out one fine day, and climbed up and up the side of the mountain until we met the gravel road. We went about a mile on the narrow and apparently little-used logging road, and then suddenly crested the top of the summit. Excitement welled up within me and tears unconsciously sprang to my eyes. Endless vistas opened up before us. We were standing at the top of a mainline, and I could see roads stretching away in every direction for miles.

Knowing what I did about logging in our area, I realized that the areas surrounding us had already been clear cut or else had immature trees, and they'd put in all these roads for harvests that had passed. We were the only souls up here, apart from the wild animals, standing on top of the world. As time passed and we continued riding over these endless miles of perfect riding territory, I would often marvel over how rarely I even saw another human soul. It would sometimes feel like they put in all those roads just for me.

What we did see was a lot of coyote scat, deer, elk, an occasional bobcat and the ubiquitous birds of prey. Amore developed a flavor for the mud puddles along a certain stretch of trail, and would always stop to drink. In the spring, small salamanders would swim in the puddles and spook her when they moved.

One other memorable day there was a sudden change in the weather that brought every garter snake in the area out onto the logging roads. It was like a snake gauntlet, and unfortunately for me I'd chosen to ride Amore that day rather than Halla. I'm guessing we broke the all time world record for the number of spooks in a single ride, as the snakes kept darting onto and off of the road in front of us for miles. Finally I just had to concede and head for home. Thankfully, we don't have any poisonous snakes in our area, so the only worry was about falling off from a spook that caught me off guard.

For the first several rides up the mountain on Halla, the horse that stopped abruptly, veered from side to side and thought that changes in light on the road were sudden drop-offs showed up again. Determined to go out alone, I realized this was a new and quite frightening environment for a horse to tackle. So I sang and hummed for quite a few rides as we adjusted, since it seemed to convince Halla that I at least was not concerned about bears in the woods, and wasn't sure why she was over reacting.

Soon we had a lovely pattern to our rides. Often we'd walk down the main road a half-mile, which rarely had traffic. Unfortunately, the traffic that did come down the road was sometimes huge logging trucks with triple trailers, and chains hanging down to rattle and bang next to us. Yet Halla wanted to be brave, and desperately tried to appear courageous, so soon would walk next to those giant beasts without a trace of anxiety as they clanked and clattered along.

Once we wove around the logging gate that marked the entrance to the mainline, I'd let Halla go and she'd gallop full bore up to the top of the hill. There was a marker at the top that said "3/4 mile" and other mile markers along the way, which was handy to know how far we were going. The barn owner had told us that this particular logging company was quite fine with equestrians using their roads. There was even a sign at the gate that showed pedestrians, dogs and horses were fine, but motorcycles not allowed.

At the top of the hill, there was a quarter mile flat area where we'd often walk or trot, and then another quarter mile hill to run up. By the time Halla had galloped a mile all told, she was ready to settle and work beautifully. We'd choose to go through the shady stand of trees to the left that wound down for a couple of miles to a dead end landing. If we went that way, there was another lovely run up a hill that Halla enjoyed. Or if we went to the right, we could go for endless miles. We'd go past a large flat rock that hung over the road and give it a wide berth, because I'd named it Cougar Drop and never wanted to find out if big cats actually sat up there. The horses preferred to avoid it.

If we went several more miles, we could climb up the Knob, a short but very steep hill that was high enough above everything that we could see the huge mountains to the south, and the town to the north where I lived that was miles away from us along the mouth of the river.

One day I went very far, past the Knob. At that point the logging road turned back and ran closer to the main paved road, and something I'd forgotten was that if you went far enough down the main road you could turn off and end up at a rock quarry. This came sharply into my memory when suddenly some dynamite blasted off. It was quite some distance away to the quarry, but still so loud and sudden as we were walking along in the absolute peace and solitude, that Halla spooked and bolted forward. What made me start laughing hysterically, after Halla slowed a few feet later and my heart stopped pounding so hard, was that I actually spooked a lot harder than Halla. If I were a horse, I'd have jumped right off the side of the road.

Another day I made a poor decision to try Halla back in a regular snaffle rather than a Kimberwicke. I reasoned that with all the galloping and running around we were doing, she felt so manageable and calm. Why did I have a curb chain and leverage on her anyway? That day we went up past the Knob, and had a beautiful ride with me congratulating myself on getting Halla to the point she didn't need a stronger bit. She was so light, and responded to just a touch to slow down.

Just past the knob, there was a crackling sound in the bushes and from my elevated position, I saw the horns of some of the big elk sticking up in the air as a herd of elk moved through the thick underbrush. Unfortunately, Halla was not able to see the horns, nor identify what type of creature was creating such a ruckus. It sounded like something massive coming toward us as the herd moved along.

She turned, and we headed toward home at a brisk trot-trying-to-become-a-gallop. We were back at the endurance ride, but this time I had less leverage in her mouth to work with. It was incredible how she moved out, and I am guessing it would have looked gorgeous on video. Her legs were lifting high and spanking along. I knew if I let her break out of that trot she would be galloping. I also knew that this gallop would continue down the very steep hills we were about to traverse, and without a doubt staying on through that type of motion was above my riding ability.

So we trotted. Down the steep hills, with me desperately trying to crank on the snaffle that sat quite comfortably in her mouth. After a couple of miles, I could feel her anxiety level coming down, but now that she was going she was quite happy to keep trotting. And she knew that this piddly little bit was never going to make her stop trotting. She probably knew that it would not stop her from galloping either, but thankfully she was in a mood to work with me that day.

My mood was a bit tense, frankly, as we trotted briskly down the side of a mountain, slipping a bit here and there as my mare cheerfully continued onward. We zoomed through the tight space around the logging gate and just missed busting my kneecap. We trotted down the asphalt road, breaking my strict rule to only walk on the road and the last half-mile home. We came trotting into the barn driveway, Halla pulled up in front, and I promised myself I would never ride her in a plain snaffle again (which I would forget someday, due to my optimistic nature).

One day I decided to try riding Halla bareback around the small loop behind the barn owner's house. The barn owner had a bareback pad, which she loaned me, and it seemed it would be fun since Halla was well used to cantering up the grassy slope near the beginning of the trail, and then casually trotting and walking the rest of the loop.

Halla's back was flat and wide, and her barrel a symmetrical shape. Since I'd ridden with a bareback pad on Amore many times, I didn't understand how the pad might react. Amore was shaped like a light bulb or a pear, with a narrow girth and shoulder area. While a saddle can slide forward going downhill, it is nearly impossible for anything to slide backward due to her shape. With Halla, however, as soon as we started to canter up the grassy hill, I felt the bareback pad begin to inch backward. After four strides, the pad was all the way back over her flanks, and now in exactly the position of a rodeo bucking strap.

We continued to go up the hill, but instead of cantering, Halla was now bucking. I'd allowed the pad to slip past me on its journey toward the flanks, so now was sitting in front of it near Halla's withers. Halla was not a talented bucker like Amore, and each stride was just a large humping leap forward. I'd already leaned forward and wrapped my arms around Halla's neck, knowing I had no leverage on her slippery sides and waiting for my seat to inevitably get shifted to the point of falling off.

But we just continued leaping up the hill. It was like getting stuck in a never ending loop, with me waiting for the bucking to get worse and for me to fall, or for her to stop bucking. Yet neither happened. It went on for so long, I found myself giggling. Although I wasn't falling off, the hill was very long, we were barely progressing, and it required a lot of strength to stay on. It was impossible for me to regain an actual seat, so eventually I decided to just roll off in the grass.

Halla kept humping up the hill, but I ran and caught her rein, and then pulled the strap to let the saddle pad slip off. She seemed very relieved to get out of the cycle.

One hot and sunny day the barn owner told me to take her Quarter Horse mare, Fancy on a bareback ride around the fields. My horses had each been out on a hard ride the day before, and I had commented that I felt they could use the day off, but yet I still felt like going for a ride.

"You can hop on Fancy," she offered. "She is like riding on a comfy couch and needs the exercise."

The eighty acres behind the smaller horse pastures were fenced around the perimeter, and a few horses were turned out there on "pasture board," which meant the owners just left the horses out for weeks at a time. Since it was part of the main farm property, we were allowed to ride on the acreage, and there was a dike around the lower fields that ran along the river. I decided to ride Fancy around the dike trail, hoping to catch a cool breeze off the river.

"Better bring a crop along, she is out of shape," Fancy's owner advised.

Fancy did feel like sitting on a pillowy sofa, her well-padded back absorbing the motion when I asked her to trot, which for her was a slow and fairly motionless western jog. It was like sitting on one of those giant exercise balls and gently bouncing up and down. She didn't need the crop to get going, being a good-hearted mare who wished to please, and still young enough to have some energy.

After crossing the upper acreage, we ambled down the pebbly hill that led to the dike. Passing through a line of tall conifers, I saw that the resident horse herd was congregating near the entrance to the dike trail. One gelding raised his head when he spotted us, and immediately came trotting briskly over, tail flagged. He didn't slow down as he drew nearer, so I raised the small crop I was holding in my right hand to make sure he planned to stop before crashing into Fancy.

The gelding was acting too interested in us, very excited. He rushed around Fancy, and thrust his head toward me.

"Back off, buddy," I said, lifting the crop again. He stopped for a moment, and then came running back into my space. He nearly bumped into Fancy, who began to tense. I warned him off, and then turned toward the dike trail.

Once on the trail, our too friendly gelding followed us onto the dike, and a couple of his gelding minions came trailing after. Soon I was directing an orchestra of noses, keeping this one and that one away from my mare, and threatening them with the crop. The overly assertive one got a whap from me, which helped him back off enough to where I didn't feel like Fancy was going to get pushed off the dike or into the river.

The other large group of horses did not follow as closely, but did migrate across the field along with us as we made our way around the dike. I hadn't realized that going out for a ride on the acreage would mean being accosted by a large group of overly friendly and little handled horses. I'd assumed they would either be mildly interested and notice us from far away, or else would ignore us altogether. Instead, Fancy and I held the group at bay until finally we exited and managed to not let any escape through the gate with us.

CHAPTER EIGHT

Turned Up Heat

Another very hot day I decided it was not good riding weather. What appealed to me was the thought of walking Amore and Halla two miles down the road to where the boats launched into the river. In my imagination, two very grateful horses would walk down the gentle slope into the river, and I'd hold the leads while they splashed and cooled off. Then we'd all walk home again.

Walking along the blacktop road was hotter than I thought. It wasn't long before the horses were sweating a bit. By the time we reached the river, the horses were quite hot and it seemed my plan would work out perfectly.

"Go on, go into the water."

My plan had not included going into the water myself, since I planned to keep my riding boots on and walk back home with dry feet. The boat access was gravel, so not appealing to bare feet.

Neither horse would enter the water. Soon I found myself behind Amore, trying to push her forward while she resisted with all her might. I splashed some water on the horses, and finally forced them to take a couple of steps, but they stood only pastern deep and wanting to get back out as soon as I would let them. Neither horse would lower her nose and take a drink either.

Well, so they hadn't wanted to cool off after all. At least we had a nice walk.

Now the sun was very high overhead, and it was getting even hotter. It seemed horses had sweated all over their bodies, and I found myself walking between two very hot beings that were also sticky and wet. A car came whizzing around a corner, startling Amore. Both horses plastered themselves close to me, smooshing me between two slimy shoulders.

We continued walking, and the slick horse coats managed to touch me at least once or twice every minute. Often when we walked, my mares would range out to the side when I was leading both of them together. Today they seemed content to walk very close and continue baking me in their combined body heat.

By the time we got back to the barn, I was sticky with horse sweat and my own sweat from head to toe. It was all over in my hair, even.

Although it was so hot, the mares acted like I was punishing them when I hosed them off, and stood dripping and sad with hanging heads while I hosed myself off even better.

A good roll in the dust soon fixed the horses' moods and they recovered well enough within moments to gallop off to meet their friends in the pasture. I skipped the roll, myself.

Although the grassy hills behind the barn owner's house were a lovely shortcut to meet up with the logging roads, there was one problem. When the grass grew nearly to the horses' shoulders, as we cut across the land, quail would often be hiding in the tall grasses. We'd startle them up, but they wouldn't break until they were right under the horses' noses. This would often spook the horses violently, especially Amore.

Somehow I'd always forget about the quail.

In the hazy afternoons or misty evenings, the hills were so peaceful, so quiet.

At the barn I'd be saddling up a horse and think, "Now don't forget about the quail." Then my horse would toil up the steep part of the hill, and I'd focus on staying out of the way and helping with the balance, and then we'd go through the shady section where the scent of tangy clover would tickle in my nostrils. The ferns would wave gently as we passed through them and the foxgloves would rise up in towers around us, as tall as the horse's shoulders. By the time we passed out into the grassy field, all I would be thinking was, "Ahhhhhh." Complete peace and relaxation.

"Flop-flop-cluck-cluck!"

Boom! The quail would explode up in our faces. Then my "Ahhhhh," would turn into "AHHHHH!"

Halla was a super smart horse, and always trying to be more brave. After a few episodes, she would perhaps scent the quail or hear them rustling with her sensitive ears. The quail would burst up, I would nearly fall off my horse and clutch my chest, and Halla would continue walking calmly. I swear she was laughing, feeling superior that I was spooking at a silly bird and she wasn't.

But Amore, of course, would never adapt to something like that. So Amore and I would always have a joint heart attack together.

After a time, the pasture-boarded horses were moved off the eighty acres and a few cows turned out on the land instead. The cows would allow us to pass through unmolested, so when I wanted a shorter ride I would often ride Halla or Amore around the dike.

When we reached the end of the river and the dike, the trail turned into a dirt road that was used to drive trucks or other equipment down to the lower fields. This road went up to a giant red barn that was part of the property, and sat empty most of the time. It was sometimes used for hay storage.

Unbeknownst to me, the barn owner had bought some pigs for her son to raise as a 4-H project, and was keeping them at the big red barn. There was no room at the main horse barn for pigs, and she wanted to keep both the noise and pig manure away from the boarders. For some reason many horse people think horse manure smells just fine, but believe that other types of manure such as pig and cow manure smell offensive. I happen to share this opinion.

Taking the dike one day, I was escorting a fairly timid rider on her Arab gelding. Sanjinn had always been an arena horse, and started in a curb bit. I'd taken him out several times to get him used to the trails for her, and found that he did not understand direct reining at all, and also lost the ability to neck rein without the comforting walls of the arena. He was a little sketchy on the canter, still hopping into it on hilly trails.

I'd told Sanjinn's rider all of these things, but had managed to convince her to come out for a simple trail ride around the dike with me and Halla. All had gone beautifully, the horses seemed relaxed, and now I thought it would be great to canter up the hill toward the big red barn as our grand finale. We started into the canter, Sanjinn hopped a couple times and then settled. Looking back, I thought his rider was managing just fine.

That was when the pigs came running around the corner of the barn, squealing.

Still looking back at Sanjinn, all I really knew was that somehow Halla went from midway up the hill to the red barn to all the way up the hill, around the corner and onto the road in just a few seconds. I was cantering beautifully, and then I saw a flash of barn, felt scrabbling, twisting, trampling feet, and whew! Standing on the road. Sanjinn was right there next to us too.

Of course the horses were not merely standing, they were transformed into chiseled marble statues with veins popping out, huge, bulging eyes and flared nostrils.

I didn't even know what had happened, but now I saw the pigs come trotting up to the fence.

Obviously, now that the horses saw that these were just small, herbivorous animals, they calmed down immediately.

Right? No, both horses turned and shot off down the road, and we didn't calm them until we had gained quite some distance from the pigs.

After that, I tried bringing the horses over a couple of times to get them used to the sight and smell of pigs. Something about the smell, I guess, but they just could not get over them. Every time we saw the pigs we had to bounce around and think about the many ways pigs could maim and kill horses.

Sanjinn's rider did not want to ride that way again, but it wasn't long until the fair came around and the pigs were sold.

I needed some new stirrup leathers because I had bought a brown saddle and all my leathers were black. Classic equestrian problem. Online, I found some leathers that were new but quite cheap. Leathers consist of a thick piece of leather, stitching, and metal. It didn't seem like there was much that could go wrong, so I went ahead and bought the discounted leathers.

When the leathers arrived in the mail, I thought the color was sharp and the stitching was tight. Slipping them onto my stirrups, I hooked them onto the saddle and took Halla out for a ride.

We walked down the blacktop to the logging road entrance, wove around the yellow gate and then I let Halla go. She galloped madly up the first three quarters of a mile, and then we trotted briskly down the flat part of the trail. As the next hill rose before us, I got up in two point and let her gallop off again.

Halfway up the hill, my right leg suddenly dropped five inches and I could feel my stirrup banging loosely before it fell off and hit the ground. My balance was not ideal, but after several more strides I pulled Halla up and managed to get her slowed before the very top of the hill. Throwing myself off the saddle, I went back to find the stirrup and discovered that the new stirrup leather's buckle had broken in half, right through the thickest part of the metal.

It could have happened at a far worse time, and I was quite happy we'd been on a straightaway after our first gallop was already over and the first flush of energy gone. Immediately I went home and bought myself an expensive and well-reviewed pair of name brand stirrup leathers.

CHAPTER NINE

Girls and Games

Dawn, Lynn and Shania lived two hours away down the coast, but on occasion they would trailer their horses up to visit and ride with me. One day they came up and brought their giant, bouncy ball so we could play horse soccer in the arena. They'd seen people playing horse soccer at a horse expo, and been training their horses to run and push the ball. My horses had not tried it yet. Amore did not think it was fun to try to touch something as unpredictable as a rolling ball, and spent more time trying to get away from it than trying to push it.

Halla began picking up on the idea, but after a few minutes we got on Cassie, Booker and Sage, all of whom were good at pushing the ball around and enjoyed it. It seemed quite fun and I wished we lived closer to one another so we could play more often.

I'd started having a teen girl come out to ride Amore, so I could exercise both horses together. I'd given her some lessons, and she did very well staying with Amore. She was a very quiet and easygoing person, with a sweet personality. She also brought snacks and drinks whenever she came to ride with me, which was a bonus. Her only flaw was that she was so quiet that I had to pay attention to see if anything undesirable was going on during our rides. For example, I happened to glance back one day when trotting the horses up a steep hill, and noticed that the saddle had slipped over to the side, and Gail was still trying to ride up the hill while listing heavily toward the ground.

Another day I hadn't realized Amore had spooked behind us but looked back to see that Gail was trying to steer her out of the clump of bushes she had leaped into. Apparently, my excitement over riding was a little concerning to Gail's mother. With trepidation Gail told me her parents did not want her riding bareback, and also did not want her to gallop. I did my best to follow these instructions, although on occasion the horses did slip into a gallop and we pretended it didn't happen.

One particular day, Halla was very relaxed and mellow. After we'd ridden about three miles, we had gone for several canters on the mountain logging roads and finally let the horses run up the steep, twisting trail about a quarter mile long that we called the Knob. Perhaps there was a little accidental galloping involved due to the grade. The steep little hill dead-ended off one of the logging roads, and had a great view from the top all the way to the rivers and towns far below.

At the top, I decided Halla was feeling so mellow that Gail should give riding her a try. I'd let her get on Halla in the arena several times before. So we swapped horses and I helped her onto Halla before hopping on Amore.

Halla walked for several steps, and then just took off trotting away down that super steep hill. Halla was never a smooth trotter on her best day, and rivaled some of the roughest, bumpiest horses I've been on. Down this steep grade, I could see it was absolutely punishing. The teen wasn't bouncing as much as she was jack hammering down the mountain.

I shouted encouraging words about checking Halla back, keeping her weight in the stirrups and other nonsense, but all the while I could see Halla's tail swinging gaily back and forth and her hips ricocheting up and down as she powered her way down the hill. The teen's helmet was thrashing around. I started hollering things about trying not to bite her tongue off.

Meanwhile, Amore, the superb downhill horse was sashaying smoothly as she sprang along behind Halla, making my ride easy. At the bottom I pulled up Amore and jumped off in order to help the literally shaken rider off her horse. She was quite relieved at the prospect of getting back on Amore.

When I got on, Halla leaped into a trot immediately, ready to take off as happily as she had for the last rider, eager for more of the fun slamming-the-rider-around. When I actually did check her back, I could feel her disappointment, and she tried once more before settling into her prior mellow mood for the several miles home.

I certainly did not tell Gail's mother about the day I made a bad judgment call. It had frozen during the night, but then warmed up enough to rain for a while. By the time Gail and I went riding in the afternoon, the skies were a usual Oregon gray and there was no wind, so it seemed to be a normal day for riding.

42

If we went up the logging road that attached to the main road that went by the barn, we could either do an out and back, or we could make a loop of several miles that ended on the trail behind the barn owner's house. On the hill just above the house, there was a very short section that was steep, and made of clay. Although the clay could churn up into mud sometimes, I'd never had the horses slip going either up or down this section, even in the rain.

What had happened was that the wet clay had frozen, and with the melting ice and rain had become far more saturated than usual. It was now as slick as snot; a fact that was quickly noted after Halla had barely set her front hooves on the hill. This trail was very narrow, and twisted between thick forest so once you were on it, there was no way to abandon ship. As Halla's hooves began slipping down the hill, I hollered back at Gail to jump off and not try to follow us down.

Halla thought quickly and sat her rump flat on the ground. I'd never sat on a horse like that before, with the hind end sunk clear down underneath me. I've gone down some steep hills where horse hunkered their hind ends well under, and even skied with the back legs, but this was crazy. Halla propelled her front legs forward as we slid, and we flew down the hill with her sitting on her bottom. Once we hit the flat, Halla's hind end sprung up, and I hopped off. Then I had Gail release Amore so I could catch her at the bottom, while Gail tried to make it down the hill herself without splatting on her face. Amore did not sit, but flailed her legs crazily in every direction, and did not topple. Gail's feet slid out a couple of times, but she caught herself on tree branches and other vegetation. After that we avoided going down that hill after a freeze.

Up on the mountain one day, I was cooling down Halla after a great ride when a large diesel pickup with two men inside came rattling by. It was unusual to see anyone up on the logging roads, and I looked curiously at the truck while they slowed to an idle next to me. They wanted to know if there was any way off the mainline in this direction, but unfortunately I had to tell them there were only closed gates, so if they did not have a key, they would only get off the gravel roads by going back the way they came.

As we spoke, the man interrupted himself abruptly to ask, "What is wrong with your horse?"

Puzzled by his question for a moment, I realized Halla's hooves were moving restlessly, and I'd subconsciously circled her back around in the direction of the truck in order to stay in a close enough vicinity to keep talking. She wasn't one to let the grass grow under her hooves on a ride.

I laughed, "She's an Arabian. They have a lot of energy." It amused me all the way home to think about what a person might expect to see from a horse and rider, and that we did not fit into that norm.

CHAPTER TEN

Knees

Until now, our story had been a happy one. At that moment in time, I felt like I had the best horse in the world to ride, and planned to keep riding Halla for the next ten years or so, until old age forced her retirement. She was fit enough to do another endurance ride, and my friends and I were thinking about entering one. Dawn and I were discussing plans one day when she came up to visit. She didn't trailer a horse up, and was just in town to do some shopping for the day. Although Dawn was a lot taller and heavier than me, Halla was a short-backed, muscular little powerhouse. I thought we could go for a short ride on the mountain trail, I could ride Amore and we could enjoy each other's company while riding through the forest.

As I suspected, Halla had no trouble cantering up the steep mountainside while carrying Dawn. At the top, she was not breathing hard at all, and wanting to trot off. We just walked, since we wanted to talk and catch up with each other's lives.

After several miles, we turned the horses back, trotted a little more and then continued walking toward home. Soon we came to the top of the steepest section of the gravel road.

The road was very dry and a little dusty, but it did not occur to me that there might be any danger. However, as we started down the hill, Halla's right front hoof caught suddenly behind a rock that was much larger than the rest of the gravel. She was wearing hoof boots to protect her soles from the rocks. When her right hoof caught, Halla threw the left front out to catch herself, but since the road was so dry the hoof slid far out to one side and she was caught in an awkward pose, quite off balance.

Apparently due to the heavier weight of her rider, Halla decided the best thing to do would be to drop to the ground on her knees. Since we had been walking so slowly, on such calm horses, Dawn had left the reins fairly loose, and although she had shortened them quickly when she felt Halla stumble, she had not been able to correct Halla's balance before she went down. Being a good rider, Dawn was sitting in the saddle as Halla kneeled, and preparing to quickly hop off.

Everything was happening in the space of several seconds. As soon as Halla's knees touched the ground, the steepness of the hill, dry and slippery footing, and weight of horse and rider combined with one another. As a result, horse and rider slid down the hill about three feet with Halla on her knees. The slide stopped, Dawn stepped off quickly, and Halla staggered back to her feet.

By now I was leaping off Amore, and saw that Halla's knees were injured badly and bleeding profusely. She'd scraped all the tissue off the front of the knees, down to the joint. Although I am quite used to the sight of blood and trauma in my job as a nurse, seeing my horse in this condition made my stomach drop and I found myself suddenly dizzy and nauseous. Thankfully, Dawn was there to provide a steadying force and sound mind.

Halla attempted to hobble a step and stopped.

I was panicking, knowing the gate below was closed, knowing it would take a long time to get a key for it and get a horse trailer in. My first thought was that Halla had broken one or both of her legs, and that the injury would be fatal. My second thought was that I didn't want her to suffer badly while we were trying to get her help.

Dawn was there.

"First, let's see if she can walk. She is putting weight on her legs, so chances are good that she can at least walk down to the road."

Her logic calmed me. Halla began to limp along slowly, but she was able to move forward one step at a time.

"Let's try to get her as far as we can while she has some adrenaline helping with the pain," Dawn said.

A short while after this incident, Dawn went to school to become a nurse, like me. As you can tell, it was a natural fit for her. She is an excellent person to have around during an emergency.

We slowly began moving Halla down the trail, and Dawn tried to see if we could get cell service. There was no reception, but I knew the phone would work down at the main road. It wasn't long before Halla was moving a little more smoothly, and her legs were not bleeding quite as badly. It still seemed like a serious injury, but I thought perhaps her legs might not have any fractures. After a few more minutes we reached the road, and I was soon able to call the vet. She said she would be on her way out immediately.

We made it all the way back to the barn, Dawn hugged me out of the shaking tremors and tears, and we hosed Halla's legs off to prepare for the vet. Halla was also a bit trembly, but was stoic as well. When the vet arrived, she gave Halla an antibiotic, pain medication, and probed inside the wounds. She said that although the injuries were very serious, it did not appear that the joints had been compromised, so the knees should heal. The biggest issue would be scar tissue, and perhaps some traumatic arthritis further down the road. But it would be a long, slow healing process.

Dawn felt terrible about the whole thing, and wanted to blame herself for being too heavy of a rider for Halla. To me it seemed that perhaps the reason Halla went all the way down was because Dawn was heavier, but there was no way of knowing if that were the case. The biggest part of the accident was the rock that tripped Halla, and the slippery footing with the dry dust underneath shallow gravel, along with the very steep grade. It was something a person would not have expected or been able to predict. Perhaps Halla would have gone down with any rider. So before she left for home, I firmly told Dawn that horses are accident prone, suicidal maniacs – always trying to "off" themselves. She was not to blame.

One problem with Halla needing frequent vet care was that she had developed a serious needle phobia. It wasn't her fault, we'd had a new vet come in for a year or so, and this vet had done Halla's teeth floating. The vet was nervous around horses, and when she didn't get the vein to inject the sedation on the first jab, she'd tried again two more times unsuccessfully. At that point, Halla had gotten quite worked up, but for some unknown reason I let the vet keep trying and she poked for a total of seven times before finally getting into the vein.

I hadn't thought a whole lot about it afterward, but the next time a vet showed up and pulled out a syringe, Halla's head and tail came up, and then she began snorting and spinning in circles. That's something to avoid, giving a hot-blooded horse a serious phobia. This new vet had treated Halla once before, and I'd explained about the problem. She'd been very patient and had managed to get the needle into the vein while Halla and I circled around her. However, now there was no choice but to give Halla lots of shots, so we needed her to get over the issue.

On the first day, Halla was very good, probably in mental shock and too much pain from the injuries to react to the needle. After that, things were not as smooth, so I spent time pretending like I was poking her with a needle, and the vet was very helpful with working Halla through the problem. In a way, the injury was therapeutic for Halla in getting over her fear of needles.

Halla was also good about letting me clean her knees and put medication on them, for about a week or so. Once the injuries began to heal, there seemed to be more nerves involved and sometimes we needed to have serious discussions before she'd let me do the treatments for her.

Serious discussions with Halla went like this:

Halla would stomp a hoof, snap her teeth or swish her tail, warning me that if I touched her she would be forced to injure me.

"You are not going to bite or kick me."

Oh yes, I am. Her eyes would flash.

"Oh no, you're not." Firm squeeze on the halter, rattle of the lead rope.

Oh yes, I am. Nostrils flaring wide, she'd toss her chin into the air.

"Oh no, you're not!" I'd leave one hand on her chest with the lead rope, and lean down to move my hand close to her knee.

Fine! Snort.

All would be well unless I tried to push the boundaries by perhaps pulling on a piece of skin that was attached to underlying tissue, or spending too much time rubbing the medication in. Then I'd hear the teeth come together. Snap! I'd hastily remove my hand and apologize, "Sorry, sorry." As long as I said I was sorry, all would be well. Halla had her limits, and only a fool would have said, "Listen, horse, I'm the boss of you."

You could only be in charge of Halla if she allowed you to, and I've never been one to see the point of fighting battles you can't win.

I tried leaving Halla in a stall for complete rest for only part of a day. There was no way she would stay locked up happily, and she was stomping around so furiously in the stall I was worried she would harm herself. Even with Amore also locked up nearby. The barn owner made a small, grassy temporary paddock outside, one where my two horses could stay together but it wasn't large enough for Halla to start running around. Halla was a very smart horse, and she did not even attempt to walk fast for the first couple of weeks.

The wounds healed ever so slowly, over a course of several months. A big issue once the wounds were healed enough was dealing with the scar tissue. Since the knees were so painful and Halla did not stretch her legs out, everything tightened up and limited her range of motion. I massaged her knees to try to loosen things up, and began to work on stretches, walking and then lunging her to get more range of motion.

For a long while I thought it would not be safe to ride Halla at more than a walk again. Since her legs did not follow a full range of motion, she seemed likely to trip and fall with her new, restricted gait. However, I kept exercising her and stretching her limbs, and after a period of time she began to have more and more range of motion. Eventually I began riding Halla again, starting with only walking and then slowly adding some trot work. I did not ride her down the steep hills for a very long time.

CHAPTER ELEVEN

Herd of Horses

One afternoon my friends from down the coast came up to check on Halla's progress and brought a big group, including two of the teens Lynn had taught to ride. Since we needed more horses, I ended up taking out Sanjinn, the Arab who'd mainly been used as an arena and show horse. Dawn rode Booker, Lynn was on Cassie, Shania on Sage, and the two teens rode on Stetson and Amore. The barn owner came along on a horse named Scarlet.

Since we had all afternoon, I decided to take everyone on a seven mile ride past the knob and down another winding logging road I'd recently explored. It turned out Sanjinn would have made a stellar endurance mount, and once I got him into his big trot it was huge, stretching and smooth. I could have two pointed on that horse forever. Cassie, of course was spanking along yet still well behaved since she hadn't been on this trail so was not riled up about it.

Stetson was a funny horse, a big tall Paint with the most sensitive skin I've ever seen. A boarder at Lynn's barn owned him, the same retired, older man who owned Scout. Scout was now quite arthritic in his early twenties, due to poor hoof care and hard use for most of his life. Dawn and Lynn had tried everything to keep the bridle and bit from rubbing on Stetson, but his pink nose sunburned frequently and his lips chafed at the slightest provocation. Before our ride they slathered him with zinc oxide paste.

Stetson had tried bolting off with Dawn once or twice after he was first purchased, but she had then made him keep running, right up the steep mountainside until he was tired, and then pushed him on even farther. He was the type of horse that was frightened by the idea that a rider could keep him going after he wanted to stop, and the reverse psychology worked well for him. Now they rode him in a hackamore, which seemed to chafe less.

Stetson trailed behind a bit with Scarlet, who was also a Paint horse and a good trail horse, trained as a reiner but unused to trotting for any distance. Sage, Amore and Booker took the middle of the herd, and I kept Sanjinn up front with Cassie to lead the way.

It was a beautiful ride, with alternating open hillsides where the sun warmed our backs and kissed our faces, and shady wooded sections. At the very bottom of the trail, we turned around at a yellow, metal gate and headed back. The hill curved around gradually back up toward the knob, and it was a lovely place for a canter. We let the horses out and Sanjinn was thrilled to be running in a group of horses. I felt a twinge of regret, wishing he had been able to lead a life of this type of riding. It was obviously in his blood, as it was with my own Arabs. Cassie led, and I wondered if she was looking too excited up ahead of us since Lynn was always one to think about that type of thing a little too late. But the hill was long, and I thought the horses would tire soon.

At the top of the hill, Lynn was able to pull Cassie up, but it took some difficulty, as I suspected. Sanjinn was breathing a bit, but as Lynn would say, his engine was revving but not about to blow.

We'd talked about the gadgets people could buy for endurance training, and I'd mentioned thinking about getting a heart monitor. Lynn thought it was part of good horsemanship to be able to feel and hear a horse's energy and listen to their breathing.

She said, "Just don't ride your horse until he sounds like he's going to blow up."

It made me laugh, but there was a lot of truth in what she said. Horses have a lot of outward signs to demonstrate their fitness. An eager horse that is not sweating hard and not breathing hard is not working too hard. Horses can breathe a bit after a hard run up a steep hill, but they should recover within a minute or so. Otherwise you are pushing them past their fitness level. Horses should never seem discouraged, lower their head, sweat profusely (although they might be quite drenched at the end of a long ride in the summer), or breathe heavily for an extended period of time.

Suddenly, Dawn said "Hold up! Look at Cassie's nose!"

She had ridden Booker up close enough to notice something unusual about Cassie. We all looked at Cassie, and saw that she had blood smeared around her nostril. Dawn dismounted and went over to take a closer look. Cassie was not breathing hard and did not look at all distressed. Yet when Dawn started looking around Cassie's nose and face, there was blood around her nose and lips. When Dawn opened her mouth, she saw more blood inside.

My thoughts raced. Sometimes racehorses can have hemorrhaging from the lungs, which shows up as blood coming from the nose. It seemed very unusual since Cassie had not been overtaxed, was very fit and this had never happened before. The blood should also not be coming from the mouth.

"Has she cut herself somewhere? Is it her tongue?" I wondered.

Suddenly, Dawn's expression changed.

"What?" Lynn asked.

Dawn smiled wryly and walked over to the bush Cassie was standing next to. She pulled off a leaf, smashed it in her hand, and sure enough it turned into a red goo.

"She's been eating the leaves, standing here."

We all laughed in relief, and Cassie shook her head impatiently.

"I don't know if those are poisonous or anything," I cautioned. "Better not let her eat any more."

We continued our ride back down the mountain and to the barn, reveling in the warmth of our friendship on a sunny day.

Having two horses was great for a horse-obsessed person like me. Even when both horses are healthy and in good shape, it can make life more interesting when you can change between riding a couple of different horses. Sometimes it was fun to ride the same ride on two different horses, just to laugh at the similarities and differences. When I'd take alternating horses on the short one mile loop around through the woods behind the barn owner's house, I would notice how sometimes both horses would spot the same black log and spook at it, or how a deer might pop out at us with both horses, but one might spook and the other might not. One horse might feel lazy and slow, and the other one full of vim and vigor.

But having two horses was essential when one horse had major injuries and needed a long recovery time. It was great having Amore to ride, and enjoyable riding her more often since I'd almost always put a second rider on Amore, the easier horse to ride when I had someone ride out with me. Amore was so impressionable, that even if she might get spooky or spunky on her own, if I was there riding on Halla confidently and controlling the pace and mood of the ride, I could easily include Amore under the blanket of our mood and she'd follow right along with whatever Halla was doing. This made her easy enough for an intermediate rider to come out with us, even if they could never have safely taken Amore out on her own, or even with a different horse and rider.

Yet I was used to having two horses to ride, so my roving eye would catch on other people's horses and I'd notice the problems they were having. Then I'd offer to put in some rides, and end up working with a few of the other horses at the barn.

Magoo was a big Appendix Quarter Horse, a sweet doofus that had some trouble going down hills. I rode him down the hill by the barn owner's house, and explained to his owner that he could do it, but he did require a little balancing support from the rider. He also needed to be allowed to move out a bit, because he balanced better at a faster walk than a slower one.

Tango was a very green, young Arab. Her owner thought she was a little too flighty and wanted to push through cues. I took her out on several trail rides, and found her to be one of the most level headed Arabs I'd been on. Barely any spook at all. Her grandsire was Khemosabi, and I'd heard he was known for more of a performance type temperament, versus the hot, spooky halter temperament that Amore had received from her bloodlines. Her owner had another older Arab gelding, and he was even more mellow, so she mostly rode him and did ground work with Tango.

There were also a couple of Thoroughbreds I rode. My first ride with Jet did not start out well. A miscommunication meant I thought he'd been ridden regularly in a certain saddle, which was not a saddle he'd ever been ridden in. When I put the saddle on, I checked to see if it cleared his spine, seemed to match his back angles, and all that appeared fine. Probably my checks were not completely thorough because I believed that the saddle was his own. I'd decided to try Jet in the indoor arena for the first ride, so walked him over to the mounting block and got on.

The instant my seat settled onto Jet's back, he reared straight up in the air. I've been on horses that reared, but I'd never been straight up before with the horse's hooves pointing toward the ceiling. Since Jet was a fairly large Thoroughbred, as he lurched back toward the ground I felt a whoosh and got this sudden feeling that the top of the arena was a lot closer than I thought.

Before I had a moment to react other than throwing my weight forward, Jet touched down and it felt like he would immediately thrust himself back up again. Thankfully, there was a trainer in the barn aisle who had apparently been walking by and saw what was happening. The trainer rushed in and grabbed Jet's bridle, stopping him for the split second it took for me to leap off. A surge of adrenaline hit me and left me feeling shaky. It had been completely unexpected, since Jet was a horse that beginners had ridden.

Immediately I knew the problem was the saddle, and yanked it off Jet. He relaxed immediately. I went and grabbed my own saddle, which appeared to fit him well. After asking the trainer to hold my horse "just in case," I mounted up, Jet tensed for a half second, relaxed, and then we walked off.

Jet was a very nice boy, a good mover, and unfortunately did not stay sound. Since his owner was not using him, she offered to let me and my new friend, Mary ride him (my new friend loved Thoroughbreds and thought Arabs were what you rode if nothing else was available). But every time we lunged him or rode him more than a day, he would come up lame. He had a bony growth on his pastern where he'd been injured in the past by a rope. This would seem to flare up after each time he was worked.

Jet's owner had another Thoroughbred, ex-racehorse named Prince. Whatever Prince's body issues were, he was extremely heavy on the forehand. He'd been ridden in draw reins quite a bit, and now just leaned forward all the time. His owner wanted to take him out on the trails, so I rode him out one day to see how he'd do. Nothing he did was concerning for a rider, except it was too much work to get him going. He crept along at the walk and was apparently unable to trot more than a couple of steps or even begin to canter up a hill, since that required using his hind end. His owner was fine with how he went, and I told her he was perfectly safe for trail riding.

Magoo's owner went horse hunting, looking for a horse shorter than Magoo that she would feel more comfortable on. Magoo was around 16 hands, and difficult for her to mount. Her idea was to get a Haflinger, but she ended up buying a beautiful grulla Mustang gelding. He wasn't as short as she intended to get, about 15.2 hands. She owned a property just down the road, where she kept Magoo, and a couple of other horses, Bucky and Red. Bucky had a bad knee, so wasn't really rideable, although I did hop on him once to evaluate his lameness. Red was very old. The new horse, Major was going to stay at the boarding stable so she could do some arena work with him.

Major was not difficult to ride, and I cantered him around the arena for the first time to see how he did for his owner. He was very overweight, sweet and personable, and like some other Mustangs I've met he wanted to know if I would make him do things. He didn't want to canter, so I gave him a little spank and then he remembered how. He did a little crow hop at the canter the second and third time he got into it, so I gave him a little spank each time and he remembered not to do that. I'm not sure why I knew he was a horse that needed spankings on the butt rather than other incentives, but I just did. After that he was lovely.

Major's only problem was one his owner asked me to help her with. His previous owner had difficulty with him standing nicely for hoof trimming, and her solution had been to hobble and throw him to put shoes on. When I went to pick up his hooves, Major's eyes rolled back and he started shaking. Not a good sign. We soon found out that he had learned an art few horses know, which is the art of well-aimed cow kicking. With all four hooves, he could hold them for several seconds, then he'd tremor harder and harder, and then yank the hoof away and cow kick you.

Once I already had three big bruises on my legs, there was no point in trying to avoid it. So we got the file out and worked on getting Major's hoof down to the ground again before his shakes got too bad and he decided to kick. Gradually he was letting us hold the hooves for longer, and I did some filing. Major quickly figured out no one was going to tie him up and lay him down. That had apparently been a very frightening event for him, poor horse.

Major was soon accompanying Halla on our rehabilitation rides. It suited Major's rider to go slowly, so she had no issues with our pace as Halla began to stretch the scar tissue and unused muscles back out. There was a very nice little ride we did that went up the hill and then off a side road that dead-ended on top of a taller hill that was invariably covered with some type of wild flowers.

Something that was always interesting about Halla was that she'd try to be brave and adapt to everything except running water. Unless she was truly startled, she'd puff herself up a little and saunter past something that in the past had frightened her. It was almost like she had to prove outwardly that although at one time she'd been scared of deer, or a flying flag, or a burned out stump, now she was so experienced or enlightened that she was indifferent about the danger.

This was not true of running water. Halla never attempted to pretend she wasn't afraid of running water. She wasn't nervous about lakes, puddles or pools. The roaring ocean didn't bother her. It was those tinkling trickles that wound along a roadside, the disconcerting pitch of a bubbling stream or the unpredictable splashing of a waterfall flowing over rocks that really terrified her.

During the rainy season, if a ditch filled with water and began to flow down the hill alongside the road, she'd want to walk on the farthest side possible. Even if she had to hear the water running, she quite preferred to not have to look at it.

On a few occasions, we would come cantering or trotting around a corner and Halla would pull up short – as we skidded to a halt, the sound of sliding gravel would dissipate and after a moment my ears would pick up the sound of flowing water. Sometimes I would scan the nearby scenery to try to spot the culprit, only to see that the source of concern was a waterfall coming down a hill across the valley.

On some routes that had streams or water flows show up each winter, I'd know where we would need to pause and let Halla look and listen for a moment, to make sure the water was not going to sneak up on us unawares. For Halla, coming across flowing water was the worst sort of surprise, and far more concerning than any wildlife, vehicles or terrain we might come across.

CHAPTER TWELVE

Blazing Trails

Around this time, Major's owner bought a property not far from the boarding barn. It had recently been logged, and she pointed out that with a little work a trail could perhaps be made that entered the logging roads from another area. Looking at satellite maps, it appeared that a large loop could be made in a different direction than we usually were able to ride. The only loop we had that began and ended at the barn went toward the west, and this loop would go east.

Making the trail through the logged area was a bit difficult, but my husband enjoyed getting out with me and helping move the rotting wood and cutting brambles with a machete. It was difficult to see the trail in the camouflage of the surrounding vegetation, so we used fluorescent markers. Creating riding paths for horses at ground level and the speed of a walking human is often inaccurate to what will work well for a horse moving along at a faster speed. Also, sometimes the lower tree branches that go unnoticed on foot appear quite low and dangerous when riding underneath them on a horse.

The first time I rode Halla on the trail, we zoomed right off it several times and got lost, missing the markers. It took a couple attempts at marking to make the paths clear enough to follow well. There were a lot of swampy, low areas, congested with marsh grasses that were tricky to get out of if the horse stumbled into them. The other option was to hack through piles of dead branches left over from the logging equipment, risking scratches to the horses' legs.

Soon we connected the trail with a very old and grass covered logging road that continued the loop. It was more work to clear the low overhanging trees from the old road, and to clear a path at the end of the old logging road to connect an elk trail that ran along a ridge and down a ravine to another hillside behind the barn. Eventually, it was a very nice, albeit adventurous loop.

The loop required a little refining, between my experimental rides where I tried it out. My friend Mary and I ran it a couple times to test it out, and it was about three miles long. On horseback, it did not go as smoothly at first. The first time I took Amore through the ravine, I wondered if the bottom had gathered some water that perhaps I could not see under some bunch grass. It felt quite steep coming down, so I stopped her and got off to lead her through. She ended up putting her front feet in the bunch grass, which indeed had squashy roots soaked in standing water, and in classic Amore style her front end buckled and she did a complete somersault that ended with her hind end coming up the other side of the ravine. At which point she scrambled up and shook herself off.

Grateful that I had not tried to ride through the first time, I cut some switchbacks into the banks and laid down some wood at the bottom of the ravine so we could avoid the soggy bottom. The other tricky part was the elk trail, which had a beautiful view over the valley but was narrow and winding. When we were working on clearing the brambles off it, a wasp stung me so I always tried to skirt horses through there quickly in case we ran across any more wasps.

Mary and I made the mistake one day of going down a shorter branch at the end of the grassy logging road, which was steeper than the rest. It had rained heavily, and the grass was wet. We decided to canter back up to the top, but as soon as we started I realized it was not a good idea. It was so slippery the horses' hooves were scrabbling around like a newborn foal trying to get onto his feet, and the boots started flinging off (this was the other time I had trouble keeping the Renegade boots on). Once the horses got into the canter, it was almost like they had no choice but to keep scrambling or lose their footing, so it was a tricky ride to the top. Of course, once we made it up safely, I had to get off Halla and walk back down to gather up the boots we'd lost.

One of my co-workers was given a big, black quarter horse named Chase, and she kept him at the same barn where I boarded. He had some hoof issues, so I helped keep him trimmed. In exchange, I was able to ride him if I wished. Eventually it was discovered that Chase had an issue with one of the tendons deep inside his hoof. However, that diagnosis took several years to obtain and meanwhile all we knew was that sometimes he was a little tender on one front hoof, while at other times he seemed fine.

Chase had not had good hoof care in some time, and it had taken a toll on his body. He was used to taking short strides, and the first time I went to get him in the pasture, I led him through a ditch, not thinking he'd have any difficulty with it. Either of my Arabs would have hardly noticed the dip in the terrain. Chase, however, took one step down into the ditch and stumbled onto his knees. This did not seem a terrible thing, since it was soft grass, but it took him quite some effort to get back up and then up the other side. After that I was very careful about leading him over uneven ground.

Chase was at least mostly blind in one eye, so he would turn his head a bit when going to the right so he could see the wall when going around an arena. He also would turn his head to see cars coming up behind him on the road, and if he couldn't visualize them well, he'd want to turn around. Despite this, he was not spooky and was safe for small children to be led around on or to be ridden by beginner riders.

Something quite amusing about Chase was that he could sometimes get very excited when going out with another horse, and want to race. However much he wanted to race, his muscles were tight, his movements were extremely collected and he could barely stretch out at all, so he'd go into a canter that had a very fast tempo, was very round and moved forward at a snail's pace. It was like riding on a rocking horse that just crept forward inch by inch as you rocked. Meanwhile, Chase would be snorting and breathing fire, and any other horse would be long gone in the distance ahead.

In the winter, one day Halla and I nearly had a crash. The weather was nice and clear, but as we climbed higher up on the side of the mountain, there were soon patches of frost on the grass. In the shady areas, some frost was even covering the gravel on the logging roads. My idea was to take it slow, and everything went fine until we came out on top and the sun was shining down, it was beautiful and crisp, and if there had been any frost on the road it had all melted. That was when I let Halla begin to trot out, and then pick up a canter. We came around a curve, and suddenly we were in the deep shade coming off the side of the mountain. Two steps later, I found that we had dropped two feet and Halla was cantering through the deep and well frosted grass in the ditch, having slid completely off the road sideways. I had her put on the brakes gently and carefully, and then we turned back home at the walk. Even walking, it was treacherous, and I kept feeling one or the other of Halla's hooves take a slide out from beneath us.

In the main mare herd, there was a quarter horse named Sassy who was the blustering aggressor that pushed other horses around. She was a young horse, bred and raised by the barn owner, and desensitized and exposed to everything possible from the time she was a foal. The owner could wrap tarps around her, have her lay down on command, and do other tricks.

Halla led her out on her first trail ride, and we only went about two miles. Sassy thought those two miles were so long and difficult, that for the last half mile home she lowered her chin almost to the ground and picked up her legs slowly, keeping them low to the ground, as if she had spent all day working cattle on the range.

Sassy was smart enough to take advantage of any situation. She'd sometimes break through the electric fence if she wanted to get to a patch of grass on the other side. It wasn't long before I learned to make her stay quite a distance away when I went in the field to get Amore. A couple of times Sassy lurked a dozen yards away from where I met up with my mare, pretending to graze. She would wait until the exact moment when I had both hands engaged around Amore's throatlatch, about to attach the halter with the buckle. In a second, she'd lift her head and charge straight at Amore, teeth bared, and Amore would flee in terror, causing the not-quite-fastened halter to fall off her face and leaving me in a belated attempt to sling a lead rope at Sassy as she ran off laughing, not caring what words I used to describe her behavior as she cavorted away.

Halla was not subjected to such tricks, because she was Sassy's number two mare. Sassy seemed to think of Halla as her backup, and they stuck close together. Sassy wasn't too much of a bully, and didn't leave marks on other horses, but would use extreme body language in order to ensure she was the first one to drink water from the trough, or to move a horse from a spot she wished to occupy.

Sassy might have been the loudest horse in the herd, which Halla admired, but soon her interests became divided. Another Arab mare joined the herd, and she was an older gray, which meant to all appearances she was pure white. Halla was always attracted to white horses, and had been best buddies with Cheyenne when we lived down the coast. This new white horse, Sissy, was no exception. Soon I noticed that Halla and Sissy had become best buddies, always staying close to each other in the pasture.

Halla and Amore were bonded together, and Halla would protect Amore if necessary. However, Amore was not a great friend when out in a large field, because she was so independent minded. She would not stick close to other horses, but would often range out alone to the very outskirts of the field if the grass was better, even if it meant she was quite separated from the herd and near thick bushes that other horses might avoid in case a predator might be hiding there. Having a friend that paid no attention to you was not very rewarding, apparently, because Amore was always a loner in every field of horses. So although Halla would appreciate riding out with Amore, and being stalled next to her, she would usually have a better pasture friend to depend on for fly swatting, mutual grooming, and general gossip.

In the mid-summer, one day when I asked Halla to canter, she humped up and did a small buck before going into it. This was very odd for her, since the only time I'd ever seen her buck was the time the bareback pad slipped back around her haunches. At home, when I took the saddle off I noticed a small scrape under the edge of the saddle pad. I reasoned that this might have irritated Halla, so gave it a little time to heal before riding out again.

The bucking persisted, and soon became a common occurrence when I asked her to canter. Sometimes she'd just hop forward for a few strides instead of giving me a true canter. Once I thought there might be a bee sting on her underbelly, another time I thought her girth might need washing. Regardless of what intervention I tried, she continued to throw in some bucking.

CHAPTER THIRTEEN

Deficiencies

At the end of the summer, we had some issues at the barn. Even though I loved the trails and the horses had always received great care, the barn owner was going through a divorce and some things that were very important to me began to slide. Several times I came out and found the horses in the fields gathered around dry water troughs, and sometimes the owner would show up with a few bales of hay at night to get by after completely running out. These things made me feel insecure, not knowing how things would end up with the upheaval in the barn owner's life. My husband and I were in the process of buying a house even farther away from the barn as well. Soon I discovered that a little barn next to the beach and only five minutes away from my house had openings for both of my horses, so I moved them over there.

Immediately after moving to the new barn, Halla developed ulcers. Sometimes ulcers are fairly difficult to discover in horses, but it was fairly obvious in Halla. Within three days of moving, instead of settling in, Halla started getting very worked up. When I led her around the perimeter of the field to let her get used to the surroundings, she began bouncing up and down like a pogo stick and after a short walk she was completely drenched in sweat from her ears to her tail. One of the boarders saw us coming back toward the barn and was quite alarmed by Halla's appearance and behavior. I reassured her that Halla just needed settling in time.

Although Halla was habitually one to give aggressive body language toward other horses, she always was full of bluff and would never actually bite or kick other horses. The next day, I saw her grab some flesh on another horse, and thought she must be very insecure in the new environment. I also noticed she hadn't eaten much of her hay during the night.

My friend April who had boarded at the other barn had some of the same concerns about her horse's care, and moved her mare Rebel to the same barn several days after I moved my horses. Still not realizing Halla had ulcers; I asked if she would like to try riding to the beach with me. Rebel was a calm, steady mare and Halla had been to the beach a few times, so I thought they would do well and we'd take it easy the first ride.

The horses seemed fairly calm, although I could feel some tension in Halla. On the beach, there was not much activity and it seemed like we could easily go down the beach a little ways without running into anything that might be frightening for the horses. I asked April if she wanted to trot, and she nodded so I asked Halla to trot. Halla took two steps of trot, and then apparently and unbeknownst to me, the acid of her empty stomach sloshed up onto her raw ulcers.

In an instant, Halla bolted. I'd galloped many times on this horse, in open areas, through tricky footing, or with competition from other hot horses, but this was far different. This was a horse running full on in a blind pain-fueled panic, with no regard for safety. My adrenaline surged after a couple of moments when I realized we were not galloping, we were bolting. When a horse bolts like that, there is no way to do a one-rein stop, no training that can help, there's just no communication at all. It's like being in a car that's flying down a hill with no brakes.

After a few futile attempts at using a pulley rein, I took mane, sat as well balanced as I could, and watched ahead for holes in case I might be able to plow rein hard enough to miss a tumble. We went for about a mile, before we hit some pretty deep sand and Halla started to flail a bit, which brought her down to a slower gallop, and engaged her brain enough for me to rein her hard to one side and get down to a trot and leap off.

It was almost worse to be on the ground. I felt a little worried for my friend, hoping her horse had not been upset by our sudden departure, but she appeared to be on board her horse in the far distance. But now my attention was taken up by this very agitated, blowing horse that was unable to lead and I had to direct in plunging circles around my body while inching back the way we came. We ran that mile very quickly, but it took a long time to get Halla back home, upset as she was.

Back at the barn and calm, I watched my horse standing in front of her hay, grinding her teeth together as she pretended to eat it while not taking any into her mouth, and I realized what was at the bottom of all this. The vet brought us ulcer treatment the next day, and thankfully Halla appeared more comfortable after only a dose or two.

After some weeks off to let the ulcers begin healing, I now followed the rule that I only exercised Halla after first making sure she had some hay in her stomach. She was soon back in work, but the bucking she had started at the other barn was getting worse. This was a horse that always preferred to canter, but now when I would ask her she would sometimes half rear and spin, leap or plunge forward, or buck. When she got into the canter, she would quickly drop back into the trot. Even her trot felt much choppier than it ever had before.

All of this puzzled me, but I was getting a clue that something was very wrong because the horse that loved to go out was getting upset and distressed about leaving the barn to go work. It had seemed like she made a steady progression with getting over the ulcers, and was eating normally. Despite that, she appeared to be losing some weight in the hindquarter muscles. Something else was bothersome, which was that Halla was very clean every time I saw her. Halla always loved to roll, and one of my nicknames for her was "Pigpen." Even when her knees had been open and raw, she'd managed to maneuver herself down every day to grind her body into the dirt.

Over the next couple of months, I explored every possibility for whatever Halla's physical problems were. I had her tested for PSSM, RER and other genetic neuromuscular disorders, and put her on a high fat, low sugar/starch diet just in case. Despite this, it became obvious that she was losing muscle and strength. She began standing funny, like she was propping herself up on her front legs. She'd only graze uphill, never downhill, and spread her legs wide for support. I noticed muscle development along her abdomen that resembled a heave line, from using her abdominal muscles to support her hind end.

Winter was almost over. Whatever was sapping Halla, it seemed to be serious and progressive, and one day when I lunged her to see how she was moving, her hind legs slid out behind her and she fell on her belly with her legs trailing behind. This looked awkward and painful, and although my main concern was for her health, I felt sad thinking I would certainly never ride her again. It was apparent that she was not lying down at all, and her hindquarters appeared scooped in on the sides and concave. Her shoulders were looking very bony and shrunken as well.

At this point, despite all the previous reading and testing I'd done, I came across some information online about Vitamin E and how it can be deficient in horses' diets. Normally horses get adequate amounts from grazing on green grass, and store it in their bodies to get them through the winter. Although this seemed too simple of an explanation for my mare's debilitating condition, I thought back over how Halla had been on overgrazed and dried up pastures for most of the last summer, and how I'd bought into the idea that vitamins might be a waste of money, so cut out her multivitamin with high levels of Vitamin E the previous spring. It hadn't been long after that when she'd started bucking, and it all had progressed from there.

I didn't even wait for the vet to test Halla's Vitamin E levels, but had some shipped immediately and started her on it right away, still with very little hope that something so simple could be such a big issue. It was incredible how quickly and obviously the muscle weakness improved. Within days, she was standing strongly and within a week she was filling in some of the muscling in her hind end. After a couple of weeks, Halla was cantering around the pasture, and when I went to see her at night she presented herself covered with dirt and grime for me to clean off. It was incredible to see something I thought must be permanent and progressively debilitating reverse so quickly and with such a simple solution.

It wasn't long before I was able to begin working Halla and riding again. There was a slight problem, which was that while Halla had been going through all of her physical issues, she'd compensated far more than usual with her stronger shoulder muscle. Now that we were riding on the beach instead of on trails, her issue of favoring one side and traveling crooked was something I wanted to correct. Between the physical weakness and no visual barriers to keep her on a path, she'd ended up with a habit of traveling down the beach sideways. Often her head and neck would be canted to one side, and I'd be riding a horse with shoulders pointing one way and the neck pointing another.

At first, it was a ton of work to keep Halla going straight-ish rather than doing half passes in one direction, and then another as we traveled forward down the longest route possible. She once again had all the energy of the universe, so didn't mind doing twice the work of the other horses we rode with. But I wanted to teach her how to use her body evenly.

It was around this time I learned about how horses can have a larger shoulder muscle from having a lower hoof, and when I looked at her from behind I could see she had this problem. Fortunately, I had been balancing her hooves well, so they were fairly even, but she'd built that muscle back up by using her dominant side when suffering from the E deficiency. I ended up buying a treeless Ghost saddle, and working on stretches and lunging to get her weaker side stronger and her stronger side stretched out more. After a time, Halla was able to get straighter and straighter, and the more she used herself better, the more even her body and movement became.

Now we had a wonderful time, with Halla feeling great again. Of course, as soon as her strength was back she much preferred cantering over trotting.

CHAPTER FOURTEEN

Adrenaline

One day I decided I'd rather bring Halla down the hill to the lower barn instead of trying to saddle her at the rack where she couldn't see her usual turnout friends, because the other horses were galloping around, and the often present roaming elk herds were shifting around the perimeters of the fields. She was still a little fidgety down below, but I made it work and safely tacked her up.

Halla was like a dog I once had. He'd go out of his mind while waiting for you to get ready to take him on his run. He'd leap in the air, twitch, bump into things, and act like a crazy lunatic. When you clicked his leash on and opened the door, he went into working mode and was super serious and focused. Halla was the same. People would say, "You aren't going to get on that horse, are you?" She would be fidgety and excited many times when I was getting her ready, but put her by the mounting block and she'd be suddenly serious. When I swung my leg over the saddle, she would immediately be working. She would walk out steady, on a loose rein, but in working mode.

It was so cold, Halla's coat fluffed out until she looked like a bigger horse. We went down to the beach, past some kids playing jump rope. Kids have no nerves or something – I swear they can't feel cold. We went past some people with dogs, a few cars, we trotted, we cantered, and went about two miles. It was close to dark and I didn't want Halla to get too sweaty in the cold.

There was a steep sand dune we had to go up to get off the beach. The footing was shifty, tricky, and it is the downfall of many horses. Meaning, they can stay calm and docile the whole ride, but coming up that hill the devil gets into them. I've seen some buck, leap, and do other silliness coming up the hill. Amore would walk or jog it almost all the time, but at the very top she would always snort and prance for about fifty feet afterward.

Halla usually handled it better than most horses, but between the cold, sharp weather and the settling dusk, it got her going a little. I felt her energy building as we started up, and I said, "Be serious." She did try, but at the end went hop, hop, and then did some jigging after we crested the hill. Then she looked over the dune grass, and I could tell she was really hoping something unexpected would pop up so she could do a little spook or bolt. But…there was nothing, just stillness and silence. She sighed, and continued.

I got off and walked the last eighth of a mile home, and she danced next to me. I'm not sure why, but she always enjoyed prancing when I got off. She didn't pull, or try to get home fast; she just did a fancy, high-stepping jog while arching her neck and swinging her head around like she was real proud of herself or something. Maybe some people would have wanted her to walk, but to me it looked like joy, and I see nothing wrong with a horse being happy. Probably it was joy that her food and friends were waiting for her back at the barn.

I hate adrenaline. Supposedly some people like the feeling of adrenaline coursing through their body, but I absolutely hate it. The sudden squeezing in the chest, heart racing, muscles filling with blood and getting tight; the shaky, tremorous feeling when the adrenaline leaves and you're left feeling weak and slightly emotional.

There are different approaches to avoiding adrenaline in the body. My approach for years has been to expose myself to things that cause adrenaline release, until my mind is accustomed and stops reacting. As a nurse, working where patients were supposedly stable it bothered me when they suddenly stopped breathing or started bleeding out. So I moved to ICU, and then began in ER as well, trying to expose myself to all types of emergencies and traumas so I wouldn't have to react with fear or an adrenaline rush when bad things happened.

With horses, I've tried to expose myself to as many situations as possible, and to ride at all gaits. When a bolting horse scared me, I began galloping all kinds of horses. I've tried to handle and work with all types of horses, and to ride in many different situations. Horse shows made me nervous so I rode in a few of those too. It works very well to train your body that a spook or a buck is no emergency. It's helped me avoid many surges of adrenaline and to feel more confident.

However, there's one type of situation I can't expose myself to, and it freaks me out every time. Horse accidents.

One night I was in the grain room rattling a garbage can. When I stopped making noise, there was still a loud rattling going on. In a moment, I realized it was a VERY BAD SOUND. There are sounds that only can be made by very large, one thousand pound animals and this was a sound that loud.

Rushing out to the sound, the adrenaline hit me full blast and I saw Halla was stuck in her gate and thrashing to free herself violently. She had grown impatient waiting for another horse to come in for the night, had put a hoof on the metal bar, and her leg had fallen through up to her chest.

These were fairly safe gates for horses, but Halla being an Arab was panicking and thrashing her way out. After a few seconds, she pulled free and stood shaking. Her injuries were fairly minor; she was bleeding from scraping her chestnut mostly off, had taken some hair off down to the hide in several places and the right front knee had a decent abrasion.

When I walked her she wasn't lame, and thankfully was not lame the next day either. Since I believe in Murphy's Law, I am guessing since I said recently she was getting into good shape that now she would need to take about two weeks off. Ugh, the adrenaline wore off and I felt shaky and horrible, but at least my horse was all right.

I coped with this sort of thing by telling my horses what stupid dummies Arabs are and how much I wished I had smarter horses. Very affectionately, of course.

There was a mellow and docile quarter horse at the barn named Earl, but deep inside he had a naughty streak that once in awhile would come out. I'm not sure if he came by his habit of self-punishing naturally, or if it was the consequence of people reacting too strongly to behaviors from a sensitive horse.

One day, I was going to lead Earl in to his stall for dinner, but I was going to go get another horse first so decided to tie him for a couple of minutes. He knew this was going to delay his dinner, so as I led him up to the tie rack he stopped and then raised his front hoof and touched my leg with it. Immediately after doing this, he rushed backward with eyes bugging out as if to say, "I can't believe I just did that, I'm so bad!" There was really nothing more to do since he'd already punished himself so completely. I said sternly, "You know it was bad, I know it was bad, so don't do it again."

Another day I was giving Earl an apple and when I held it out to him he bit my hand lightly, which caused me to drop the apple into his grain bin. Then he grabbed the apple and rushed back into the corner of his stall. Immediately again his eyes bugged out and he cringed while standing cowering for more than a minute. In between these brief episodes of naughtiness, Earl was always well behaved and sweet, so it was amusing that he had a little devil inside that would sometimes come out, to his own chagrin.

On a calm, warm day it was a little sunny and yet the horses were spookier than anything. I tried to take Halla for a ride to the beach, but there was no beach due to a recent storm that had left behind some very high surf. We went down the dune and immediately back up after we got to the ocean, and I tried riding her along the top of the dune but the sand was so deep between the dune grass that I thought it would be easy for her to get injured by a misstep. Halla had a couple big spooks during our ride, but when I took Amore out she won the prize.

I'd given up on the beach idea due to the tide, so just rode Amore around the trails on the barn property and through the large, open fields. When we entered a trail through some bushes, Amore did this spook where she hit a gallop in one stride, then did a sideways scramble before stopping with her legs all askew.

Thankfully, I was riding in my new Ghost treeless saddle, which was so secure it was almost disconcerting. I'd ridden those spooky types of horses so long by now that I depended a lot on my body moving in the saddle as a signal to instinctively react. When Amore did that giant spook, I had her on a completely loose rein. Normally I would have instantly shortened the reins and been ready to cue which direction to turn, in case the spook turned into some type of run. Some signal to my brain went haywire since my body didn't move in the saddle, and I found myself sitting on Amore after the spook with a still totally loose rein in my hand. I thought that was not good, since I might have found myself galloping away through some wicked bushes.

The next day it was rainy, windy and rather stormy. Six people from the barn were going out riding. What nuts horse people are. Two riders stayed and worked their horses in the outdoor arena while the other four of us went down to the beach.

I was on Halla, in the new Ghost treeless saddle. Someone asked, "Hey, aren't you trialing the saddle? On the beach in the rain?" But I explained I'd already decided to keep it, and was sending the payment that day.

The wind coming from the west was cold and strong. The rain was so icy we couldn't decide if it was hail or rain, but our faces were too numb to differentiate the feeling. Yet the horses were still cheerfully heading toward the beach with Nala the Thoroughbred diving for the grass at every opportunity, Satin the Arab prancing along and Halla keeping a serious eye on both of them to keep them in line.

When we arrived at the beach the rain suddenly stopped, and as we turned north the wind faded down to a steady breeze. The sun peeked over the dark clouds and a bald eagle stood on a snag over the dunes, his white head gleaming as a rainbow spread across the sky behind him. We had been feeling we might have made a mistake to go out in the weather, but now we looked around and felt how lucky we were. Everyone else was missing this, a sight worthy of being in a painting.

Like the day before, there was still only a strip of beach due to the high, pounding surf. The foam whipping off the ocean was running in packs and some pieces were the size of basketballs. Satin, the Arab was the first to figure out that the foam bounced harmlessly off of horses. Halla took some flying canter leaps to avoid the foam before she figured it out too and settled. Nala got chased up the dunes by a pack of about twenty big chunks of foam that seemed determined to catch her. One hit her leg and she figured out these predators were illusionary too.

We continued down the beach, with Earl the quarter horse lagging behind trying to step around every piece of flying foam. The three of us in front turned after a bit and saw Earl's rider was off; apparently she hadn't ridden it out when some foam finally caught him. After she got back on, we went just a bit farther and then headed back.

Now the rain was completely gone, and Satin's rider, April began lamenting the ride was over so soon. She and I saddled another pair of horses and went out again - this time I was on Amore and she was on her own mare, Rebel. A lot of the foam had blown away by the time we made it back to the beach. It seemed clear so we decided to canter, and I got left behind when Amore had to dance around some foam that suddenly appeared. But I got her going again, and we had a nice ride, but a short one since by now it was growing dark.

Going up the dune, we were headed east and the west wind picked up sharply again behind us. Amore began to gallop in the deep sand. When we got to the top of the dune, the wind whistled around her legs and tail and she got a little too excited. She leaped in the air with all four legs, and then twisted her barrel and kicked both hind legs out to the side. It was like a capriole but with her own personal flair added. Again, the new saddle shocked me as I barely moved out of the seat. It seemed odd that a treeless saddle could be more secure than the treed ones I'd ridden in, but that seemed to be the case. April coming up the hill behind me said she thought she was finally going to see me fall off. I think she was secretly disappointed. I told her not to worry, I could fall off with the best of them.

It took several minutes to calm Amore down, she did another small bucky thing and then settled and we had a nice walk home.

CHAPTER FIFTEEN

Horse Opinions

Amore called out loudly and repeatedly when I went out to see her one night. I saw she had a typical Amore problem going on. She'd eaten her nighttime allotment of hay inside her shelter, and it was raining outside. She didn't want to go outside to graze on the green grass out there in the rain, but she also didn't have anything else to eat inside.

The other five horses that live in the same setup as Amore were happy and contented. They'd eaten their hay and were dozing comfortably inside their spacious shelters. They knew that it was their own choice to stay inside and dry and that if they wished to eat, they'd need to get wet. Amore was the only one in distress. I gave her a little more hay to make her happy.

Halla was a very opinionated soul. I found her amusing every day. For instance, if I brought an apple out and gave each horse half out in the field, I could halter Halla but she would insist that she must finish chewing and eating the entire apple before consenting to being led away. I would say, "Come on," and try to get her to hurry, but she would plant her feet and give me this look describing in detail how offensive this was, so I had to try not to be rude and wait until she was done and ready.

I finally found Halla's "spot" for saddling at the new barn. At our last barn she had a "spot" where she preferred to be saddled. Of course I could saddle her anywhere else, but doing so meant fidgeting, moving, swinging the butt around on occasion, and in general a more difficult experience. At this barn, I had yet to find that spot. But one day I discovered the perfect spot. We had to go about three feet to the right of the actual tie rack, to a pasture gate. I could drop the lead here or just throw it over the top of the gate, and Halla would stand stock-still and contented while waiting to be tacked up. Just like at the other barn, I could either argue with her every day about fidgeting while getting saddled, or I could put her in the right spot and have her be an angel. She was just very opinionated.

When I took the horses out of their pasture one day, they were quite happy, thinking I was about to feed them. The happiness turned to suspicion when I tied them up and put a bareback pad on Amore. Uh-oh, was dinnertime turning into working time?

73

Hopping on Amore, I ponied Halla next to us and the horses headed out without hesitation and much quicker than either of them would have walked out alone. Once we headed out into the big field on the west side of the property, however, the wind picked up and it began to rain lightly.

Now the horses began to question why we were out here. "What is the point?" they seemed to ask.

I thought it was funny that our three heads were so close together. Amore led, Halla walked with her head just in front of Amore's shoulder, and I sat on Amore. I told them that we were a three-headed monster.

We went through a narrow trail and Amore kicked out at Halla a couple of times. Usually this was not allowed by Halla, but for some reason Amore felt like kicking out today. Halla did not appear to be doing anything rude toward Amore, and yet Halla took it very blandly as if she didn't even notice. It was a rather feeble gesture, as fake kicks go.

We went over a log, up a steep little hill and exited the trail into a large, grassy field.

Suddenly the horses got the point of our little journey as I jumped off and gave the horses some line so they could graze. Now the rain didn't bother them and they were very happy to be out in this lush field with endless tufts of green grass. They were eating so fast the grass was bunching up and hanging out both sides of their mouths. Green grass can be a powerful mood lifter for horses.

I was beginning to realize that the beach, our primary venue for everyday riding, was very tough for horses. Where we used to ride, the trails through the woods would often stay almost the same each day. Sometimes a tree would fall down, or flowers would bloom. But we would have the same corners, the same ups and downs, and each trail was similar to another even if we went for miles. The footing was gravel or grass or dirt.

The beach is different. Some days it is a small, steep slope of shifting deep sand that is only twenty feet wide with huge waves crashing down right next to us. Some days it is a wide, flat expanse that is three hundred feet wide or more. Sometimes it is smooth and shiny. Sometimes it has deep ruts and lines all over. There can be no debris for a mile, or there can be thirty objects such as driftwood, fluttering pieces of plastic, empty buckets and shells in thirty feet. The sand can make a thudding sound under a horse's feet or it can sound like a dry rattlesnake rattle. Sometimes it makes a scuffing sound like shoes squeaking on a gym floor.

Then there are the people. They throw balls, or they jump. They ride bicycles, chase barking dogs, and fly kites over our heads. They attach fluttering flags to their cars and drive them splashing through the water. They start fires, run into the water and scream. There are helicopters that fly low over our heads. There are also shells that litter the beach at times, dead rotting sea birds and fish, and elk herds that congregate along the way to the beach. The waves come crashing in endlessly.

For a while after moving to the new barn at the beach, I wondered if I was becoming more cautious when riding than I had been in the past. It seemed there was more decision making involved and more times when it seemed better to pull horses up or not let them run full out. It wasn't long before I realized this was because of dealing with an ever-changing environment that required adjusting for all the danger factors and taking each day as it came.

On one ride, I was hesitant to let Amore canter very fast or very long. The beach was littered with hazards, she felt wound up tight underneath me. On our final canter she kicked a hind leg out high to one side so I knew she was feeling a little goosey.

Knowing that others I rode out with might want to take off down the beach, sometimes I felt bad about saying I'd like to do more trotting or to take a slower pace some days. There were many valid reasons for this, such as horses that were not in excellent shape at the moment or too warm weather with a horse still in winter coat. But I would check to make sure my valid reasons were not excuses covering for a lack of confidence. But honestly, I do believe that most of the time I successfully rode the fine line of when and where to let those hot, reactive horses' energy out, even in that type of environment, while keeping in consideration the fitness level, the tripping hazards, and safety for all.

It's another part of horsemanship, a difficult one. Knowing how to be safe without cowering in fear, knowing how to keep others safe when they have no compass for what can happen with out of control horses, knowing when you need to push yourself and your horses a bit, to find the boldness within.

The type of person I get along the least well with is the hysterical, dramatic type. Yet I've learned that dramatic, hysterical type horses are just my thing. I find them highly entertaining.

One night I decided to ride Halla very late, after all the horses had begun eating their night hay. It just is funny how some horses don't hide their emotions and you know exactly how they feel. I brought the bareback pad out, and she was very upset about it. She stood up tall and rigid, turned and walked outside, then back into the shelter. Quite obviously this was not part of the normal schedule, it was quite unfair, and why was I doing this to her? She snorted a couple of times. Then I put the pad on and a bridle, led her outside and she stood still while I hopped on, and then went walking right off like nothing unusual had happened. Down to business. She would let me know she didn't approve; but then never hold a grudge or anything, and get right over it.

For some reason Amore was the opposite. She would have stood calmly to get tacked up, would have started off fine, but during the ride would have had difficulty focusing while thinking of her hay waiting for her at home. In my opinion, horses have an abundance of personality, but some horses, particularly Arabs even more so.

On one particular ride I went out first on Amore with Satin, the little Arabian that looked just like her. I put a double-jointed D-ring snaffle on Amore, the first time I'd ridden her in a bit for a couple months or so. Lately she'd been a little goofy at times on the beach, and sometimes the bitless seemed to feel like not quite enough control. Satin was quite energetic and "up." My friend April, who had just recently started riding Satin futilely attempted to make Satin stand still for saddling. I laughed; having been around Arabs in fidgety moods and thinking she should probably save her energy for the ride.

Amore was in a quite calm disposition, herself. She was mellow through the whole ride, and nothing bothered her at all. Light, forward but relaxed at all gaits, and balanced. Satin danced, pranced sideways and up and down. My friend was riding her in my Flower hackamore, and it was not the right headgear for the day. She had a few periods of going on a loose rein, but not many. We cantered a little and Satin had her body and legs going every which way. I wasn't sure if she was switching leads sometimes - it was more random looking like her legs were trying a few different gaits at the same time. Well, we rode about four miles and by the end Satin was going well enough.

My friend said perhaps the next ride she would try her own Tom Thumb snaffle instead. We talked about that for a while. I told her that although the bit got a bad rap sometimes, it wasn't necessarily a bad bit. However, since she didn't know if Satin had ever worn a curb, and also Satin didn't know how to neck rein, I suggested she might try a snaffle first. She said her own mare, Rebel went beautifully in the Tom Thumb. I didn't mention that I'd ridden her mare in the Tom Thumb several years ago when she'd asked me to exercise the horse when she was on vacation. Her mare objected strongly to any pressure on the bit by throwing her head forward, gaping her mouth, and slowed down jerkily rather than smoothly even though I was very light with it. Rebel was ridden often in a rope halter and definitely did not need a chain – she was a kid safe horse. But my friend's perception was that a Tom Thumb was one of the softest western bits out there, and I said that could be true if you didn't need to use a lot of contact.

On our second ride of the day, I went on Halla, and April took her own quarter horse mare, Rebel out in a crossunder bitless bridle. Another rider came with us, Cammie, who was someone I'd boarded with off and on over the years at different barns in the area. She was a very good rider, and her Thoroughbred Foxy who had passed away recently had been a wonderful, athletic horse. Her current Thoroughbred was named Nala, and she brought her out to ride with us.

All the horses went very well. After about a mile, Rebel's rider turned around and we took Nala and Halla for a gallop. I found it amusing that their names rhymed. It mixed up some people at the barn. I had some people ask if Valhalla's name was Halnalla or Nalhalla.

I wasn't sure how Halla would behave since our ride on the previous day hadn't been the smoothest. On a whim, I'd taken her out in a snaffle. That was something I'd decided a couple years before to never do again, after meeting the elk up on the mountain and trotting the whole way home at a crazy, slip-sliding speed. At that time I had decided it wasn't safe to ride her in a snaffle.

We had gone all the way down to the beach (about a half mile) totally relaxed. Then Halla had realized she only had a snaffle in. Well, she kept trying to tank off. As in, after one step of trot she would gather her hind legs and push straight off into a gallop. At which point I had to turn her tightly around and make her go back to a walk and try again. She was far too smart to go in a bit she didn't respect and just behave. She had to "believe in the bit" so to speak. But I did learn some things.

Now galloping with Nala, I had Halla in a Myler mouth short-shanked curb, and found that she was able to balance much better with a little contact for faster work. She was getting stronger, straighter than ever, and seemed to enjoy her rides very much. It didn't seem like the curb was any less comfortable than a snaffle to Halla, and with the slight leverage I was able to ride using just light pressure from my fingers on the reins most of the time.

I was wondering why I couldn't ride Halla in a snaffle when my friend rode Nala, a hot Thoroughbred in one. I think was about a difference in temperament. Nala was taught to lean into the bit, and she would take off sometimes. But she would get a fright or a spook or want to run, and not sustain it. Halla was more determined and could build up a level of excitement and sustain it. Her mind was more focused on her strong will to run. Nala had a flightier mind and would bend to the will of others, humans and horses. She didn't sustain a mood or an idea. When I rode her it felt like you could distract her out of things. She'd ask to go fast, and it would feel like she was charging off. She was a very fast Thoroughbred, with incredible speed and endurance. However, most of the time you could circle her around, or even just give a strong pull on the reins and she would change her mind.

Nala's mind felt like: "I'm soooo excited! Wheee I'm flying! Now what should we do?" Halla's mind felt like: "I'mrunningI'mrunningI'mrunningI'mrunningsofast." It was very difficult to get her out of that loop.

At this point I was discovering that Halla was requiring that I hold a slight amount of pressure on the bit. I always thought she was pushing through the pressure and trying to canter. But now after spending some time working hard on getting her to trot on a loose rein, I realized she found it very difficult. When I put the snaffle in and gave her a little contact, she found balance. It seemed that with her strong hind end push and downhill build, she found it difficult to balance the big trot with the added weight of a rider. Adding to this were the leftover issues with her knees, which she moved very well but still did not have the complete stretch to her stride or range of motion she had once had prior her to injuries. It seemed that she lacked a bit of the braking action her body needed for athleticism while carrying a rider, and if the rider provided some help with this with the bit, she was able to stretch out more and go faster.

Cammie had not owned Nala for very long, and was trying to overcome some body issues Nala had, along with teaching the Thoroughbred how to manage her energy. Being turned out with other horses and not locked in a stall was already helping make Nala easier to ride. However, she was a hot horse and had been known for chucking off riders. With both horses learning to work hard, to go faster over the open beach without losing their minds, and getting more fit, we helped each other out tremendously. The horses were very complementary to each other, and both benefited from being allowed to move out and to work hard.

One day, as we arrived at the top of the dune down to the beach, there was a large bald eagle sitting on the crooked snag where the raptors like to hang out and survey the territory below. For some reason, Cammie did not want to go down our usual beach access trail, but thought there would be better sand on the trail near where the eagle was sitting. She began to make a wide berth around the bird, but his magnetic stare seemed to draw me in, and as I looked at him I found myself riding Halla quite close to where he sat.

For some reason, I had this feeling that the bird was not afraid of us, and was not going to fly away, and although I'd been close to eagles and noted their tremendous wingspan, it didn't bother me the way it should have that we were so close. Nala drew closer as well, and suddenly the giant bird opened his wings while we were right next to the snag, so felt like we were ducking right under them. As he lifted off, Nala dropped, spun and flung Cammie right off into the sand. Halla spooked also, but I managed to stay on. Cammie was back on in an instant, and we watched as the raptor flew away, laughing at ourselves for thinking we would just skirt by a massive eagle and be on our merry way.

CHAPTER SIXTEEN

Challenges

After taking out Halla for several rides, I decided to take Amore out to knock some cobwebs off, and we ended up having a fractious ride.

Frac·tious: adjective

wayward, unruly, uncontrollable, unmanageable, out of hand, obstreperous, difficult, headstrong, recalcitrant, intractable

"The horse was frac-tious, which put the rider at great risk for frac-tures."

The main problem was of course, that Halla the Big Boss was missing. We had Nala, who could be twerpy, especially for a Thoroughbred, and Satin, the doofy Arab.

It was chaos. No one was in charge, and they decided they were a band of rogues. All was fine until we hit the beach. No one decided "let's trot now" and strode confidently forward. When we said they could go faster, the horses sort of fiddled around and looked at each other, with Satin and Amore trotting ahead a bit. No one really picked up a canter, they just kind of pattered ahead until their feet found a sort of three-beatish gait. It felt fine for a moment.

Suddenly, Nala bolted from the rear. Amore heard the change in gait immediately, and startled forward. Then the windbreaker I'd foolishly put on made a sound somewhere between a zipper opening and a tarp being beaten to death. As Nala whipped past, stretched out as beautifully as American Pharaoh, Amore's eyes bulged out of her head and she bolted into a gallop. Not a lovely-day-on-the-beach-let's-run gallop, it was a zipper-tarp-monster-is-chasing-us-we're-going-to-die gallop.

It was a strange thing. When Halla lost her mind was a super rare occurrence and it frightened me. Amore had lost her mind on a regular basis since I first met her, and I always had this odd, twisted feeling that this was not safe and I needed to regain some type of control, but at the same time I was laughing hysterically inside. Halla went crazy like a force of nature bearing down on you, a tornado too powerful to fathom. Amore went crazy like a demented clown. A little scary, but also kind of funny.

Luckily, the sand near the dunes was very soft and deep that day. I turned Amore toward it and her gallop began to thrash and churn until it slowed her down. As we slowed, the sound of my jacket lessened and I think she thought we'd left the demon behind. After I caught Amore, Nala noticed in the distance that the others were not following and her rider caught her too. Satin was feeling more directable, so stayed between the two and stopped when they did.

The rest of the ride down the beach Amore was less panicked but still frightened. I stuffed the hood of my jacket down, which tamped down the noise quite a bit. She was still trying to rush off at every opportunity, spooked mightily to one side when we passed a log, and felt rather tense.

Finally, just before we turned around, Satin's rider took her into the ocean. Amore watched them cautiously, until Satin was far enough away that the setting sun glaring off the water made the horse and rider no more than an oddly shaped shadow surrounded by brightness. At which point Satin turned around and came splashing back toward us and Amore was suddenly uncertain about what sort of creature had risen from the deep. At the sound of the splashes, she panicked and spun the opposite direction, fleeing away.

Although I can't say I almost fell off during the ride, I was getting tired of wondering if I was almost going to fall off! As Cammie said in consternation when Nala spooked on a ride, "I almost lost a stirrup!" These things disturb riders that go about on spooky horses.

So we went away from the water and walked in the deeper sand, at which point it was time to turn back home. Well, the weather looked different in another direction. Wind at our backs, setting sun on our faces, Amore grew very cheerful and relaxed. The jacket was no longer pursuing, and we did some lovely big trotting on a loose rein. Nala had chilled out too, but now Satin was wishing she could get quickly home to her dinner so her rider was unable to give her a loose rein. Well, each of us had part of a ride that was relaxed at least.

During this time period, riding Halla was often interesting and challenging. She kept getting straighter and stronger, seeming to have recovered completely from her Vitamin E deficiency, and the scars on her knees never seemed to bother her. She was getting very fit, usually doing a seven or eight mile ride at a fast pace each week, along with a couple of other shorter rides. Often when we first hit the beach, the horses would want to run, especially if we had Nala and Halla out together. Nala would usually do a power trot while Halla would canter for the first mile, if there was congestion on the beach or the sand was not great. Otherwise we might start right into a gallop, and run the horses for a mile or so.

On hot days, we would sometimes go down to the estuary, where the river met the ocean about three miles down the beach. If the weather was hot, Halla would follow Nala into the water and they would splash around quite happily. Horse hooves naturally displace quite a bit of water, so it is easy to get a horse wet and cool just by walking or trotting them around in shallows.

We would circle around the riverbank and head back toward the ocean. Now there was a wide, flat expanse of deeper sand where Cammie would usually let Nala gallop. With Halla's shortened stride from her knees, and shorter height, I would need to check to see how deep the sand was before starting out cautiously. Cammie would just let Nala go, and soon they'd be fading off far in the distance. Halla would sometimes trip a little when the depth of the sand changed, but then catch herself. If the sand was not very flat and hard, sometimes I would have Halla switch leads a few times to control the excitement level. Sometimes I would wish for a flat track with really groomed footing and no unpredictability so we could just always let the horses go and know they wouldn't trip or fall into holes.

Sometimes Halla would get too hot and I'd spend a couple miles having her turn half serpentines and switch leads every few strides. Otherwise she would have just tanked off with me. The curb bit with the independent side pieces was very nice for directional steering. It never felt like I was doing anything harsh even with the leverage when I pulled. On occasion she'd try to lower her head and tank off with me, so then even with the leverage I'd have to use a bit of my core strength and tell her "Nope," and lift her head back up.

Since Halla preferred to canter whenever she was feeling good, often she would canter along while Nala did her beautiful and big extended trot next to her. They could easily go for a couple of miles that way without even taking a deep breath. Halla seemed to think she was a racehorse. She'd go out for a gallop, then enjoy a good hosing all over, even on her face and under her belly. Then she liked to have the sweat scraper, and then some hay and oats, like a Thoroughbred. Seemed like she would have fit in on the racetrack. Of course there are Arabian racehorses too, in some parts of the world, and quite possibly that is where her lineage was from.

A coworker of mine named Sandy came to see Amore and I had her try riding mostly around the property and in the arena. She was a previous horse owner who was currently horseless after moving down from Alaska. I saw she could ride and had a good seat. So for the next ride, we took her out on Amore with Nala and Halla. Poking around wasn't going to cut it for those two, so once we hit the beach it was "go time." Since I was on the "boss hoss," I kept it down to a slow canter while Nala and Amore trotted and cantered.

We headed down a couple miles at a steady pace, onto a trail, and then back to the beach. When we came around a bluff, it didn't occur to me that the last couple times we'd gone around this corner (which opens up on a wide stretch of open beach), we'd gone for a short gallop. I was in front when all of a sudden I heard thundering hooves coming up fast behind, and then saw Nala fly by at a very fast gallop. My new friend on Amore looked quite calm, actually, and had Amore well under control as we kept cantering. I suspected that Nala's rider had not meant to go roaring off at that pace, so I told my friend we'd keep our pace down and catch up gradually so if Nala had lost her calmness she might find it again. After about a half mile, we caught up to Nala, and her rider said that she hadn't meant to take off at that speed, Nala had just tanked off suddenly.

It wasn't long before Nala was very calm, and very tired. Halla was the one who got jiggy for a while, since her pace had been kept to a medium canter the whole ride. This was also her first time out since scraping her leg a couple weeks prior, so she had a bit of extra mental energy going on. Everyone made it home without a mishap, and although Sandy was more used to larger horses, she was pleased to have a chance to come and ride Amore with me sometimes.

The next time Sandy came to ride with me, I made two mistakes with my tack. First, I tried putting a neoprene curb guard on Halla's bridle over the leather strap for added padding, and I also tried some new, wider and supposedly more shock absorbing panels on my Ghost saddle. Nala's rider, Cammie was along also, and I was optimistic we would have a great ride since things had gone well the last time.

We hit the beach, Halla noticed that the curb strap had as much "bite" as an athletic sock and we spent the first mile with me disengaging her driving end as she tried to gallop off. That was when I noticed the wider panels under the saddle did not work for Halla's flat shape, making the saddle easily slip off center.

After a mile I got off and took the neoprene guard off the curb strap. Something I'd learned about Halla was she only gave as much respect as she believed I could enforce. Although I've only been around nice and gentle studs, I could imagine she might have been similar to a stallion in that you had to prove to her that you could manage her, otherwise she would happily walk or run all over you. But the instant you had everything going for you, she became manageable and compliant with a workmanlike attitude.

I struggled with the saddle slippage for the entire eight mile ride and kept Halla down to a controlled canter. At the six mile point, Amore began slightly limping at the trot only. Back at the barn we found a point on her hip (seemed to be favoring her right hind) where perhaps she'd been kicked at some point recently, and apparently the ride had made this injury sore. At home she was quite lame at the trot so I had to give her a few days off to see how she did.

Amore's new rider handled her beautifully. I asked her if she wanted to ride again while Amore was recuperating if we found her another horse, and she was all for it. Cammie was free, so we took Nala, Halla and Satin out together.

We also started the ride with Earl, the quarter horse since his rider was tacking up when we arrived. We tried for about a mile or so to keep Earl going with us, but his walk and trot were so slow compared to the hot bloods that he kept falling farther behind. Finally we asked his rider if she wanted to keep going or go back, and she decided to head back. That was fortunate since Nala was extremely keen and fresh despite an eight mile ride on the previous day. Once we left Earl and began galloping, Nala did the most hilarious leap during her gallop. It was as if she threw a long jump in for fun. We were keeping Satin and Halla back behind a bit, and both Satin's rider and I busted out laughing at Nala's antics.

Halla was overjoyed from the start. First, she saw there were three horses going out and she grew two inches taller at the thought of being in charge of such a big herd. On the beach she locked her gaze onto Satin while keeping a watchful eye on Nala too. I honestly believe she thought she was controlling the other horses as we sped along. She didn't seem to care about losing Earl too much, perhaps it was enough responsibility to have the other two horses.

I'd put the good panels back on my saddle so had a secure seat, and fixed the curb. It took Halla about five seconds to figure out I was in control when we hit the beach and then she was instantly cooperative.

Sandy had an excellent seat and hands, as well as a very good feel for when to hold back and let a horse out. Satin was very excitable and I kept asking her rider if she felt comfortable with the situation. She said she hadn't really ridden hard in a few years due to her last horse's aging, and had never galloped much. But she was obviously bold and our galloping did not phase her, and she let Satin out and drew her back to keep her engaged without losing her mind. That can be a tricky skill and I was pleased about happening upon another good rider to go out with. By mile six, Satin was walking toward home nicely on a loose rein and with a soft eye.

Another day I went out and took Halla for a lovely canter down the beach, just the two of us. All went well until we came back to the dune where we accessed the beach, and I saw that someone was standing just below and flying a kite, one of those that could be steered with your hands, and that made a loud buzzing sound as it whipped through the air. Although I hadn't done so previously, I decided to go up the beach access that was about two hundred yards more north than the one we usually took, in order to avoid potential trouble. Unfortunately for me, it turned out someone had placed several plastic beach chairs on the dune, and they were well hidden from view by the tall beach grass until we crested the hill, at which point they popped up in front of us.

Halla spooked violently at the chairs, and I stayed on although my seat was just a little off kilter. Unfortunately, my weight had slipped toward the downward side of the steep hill we were still on, and Halla began lurching toward the upward side of the hill. This caused my weight to slip a little more off with each stride, and although I tried valiantly to throw my weight up, the plunging forces and gravity eventually won. The sand was so deep it sounded like "poof" as I dropped into it, sending up a cloud around my body.

My horse ran, and I ran after her. Since we were slightly off our usual route, Halla ran straight east and into the neighborhood next to the one we usually rode through to get to the beach. After passing the first house, I saw that she had ended up in a fenced back yard, which had trapped her, and she was now standing looking very confused and forlorn, but thinking about trying to start eating some of the green grass that surrounded her. Gathering up my horse, I snuck her back out of the yard and led her briskly back to our usual route, hoping no one from the neighborhood had noticed our invasion.

CHAPTER SEVENTEEN

Trips

Although I'd promised myself not to use a snaffle on Halla again, I did try a Waterford mouthpiece on her one day. Supposedly they are very good for strong horses, since they don't allow the horse to lean. She found it very gentle and tried to take off once we started going faster. When she discovered it wasn't quite as gentle as she first thought, she became angry with it and tried about five different types of evasions. None of them worked perfectly for her, but I found it took a lot of strength to stop her. Those who say to be careful or you'll teach a horse to run through a Waterford? Well, Halla was sort of genius with bits and figured out very quickly how they worked and if she could get around that.

Cammie had read lots about Waterfords too, and had some suggestions about different ways to use it. Halla didn't "lean" or put her head down. I think that's why it didn't work for her. I was thinking of her as one that leaned, but now I realized she didn't actually lean. She very rarely had a heavy feeling with the bit, but she could arrange her body behind the bit and push from behind very powerfully, and then in order to manage the speed and direction I had to use contact and release that she respected. So since she didn't actually use the bit to lean on and propel herself, the Waterford mouthpiece was too gentle when I contacted her with it, and she didn't respond easily or lightly.

Every time it seemed like things were going well, something would come up to throw a wrench in the works. Amore had been lunging well and I'd taken her on several short rides where she felt perfectly sound. So on a beautiful, sunny, windless day Sandy came to ride her again. Halla, Nala, Satin and Amore all headed down the beach to the estuary. After our little sandy dune trail, we circled back and then it was just pure beauty with gallops, Nala zooming all over the beach with her gorgeous gaits we all admired, splashing into the ocean, sun and sand and horses. The stuff dreams are made of.

As we headed back, Amore's rider kept saying Amore felt off, but it was so difficult to pinpoint what was wrong. Was it right hind, left hind? I kept thinking her back movement seemed stiff. Sandy kept trying to get Amore to work over her hind end, but Amore was resisting and going behind the contact. I should have said, "Let's walk back," but we were having such a lovely time! The nagging off ness was not obvious, and I knew Amore was in heat which often makes her act oddly, and I now did not believe it was the hip we thought it was, since I had not been able to find an issue after all kinds of prodding and flexing.

So I hung back a bit with Amore, and we didn't push the pace but caught up now and again. We were just coming to the end of our ride, Nala and Satin went off to go in the ocean one more time, and Halla and Amore began a very slow canter. I looked back to see if Amore looked sound, which she did, and as I watched Amore fell down flat on her chin. We were on a perfectly flat, smooth surface, but she tripped, went to her knees, then laid out flat and tipped her rider forward onto the side of her helmet, knocking her out cold for about a minute.

Thankfully, there was a couple in a parked car taking photos as we went by. They jumped out and I told them to call 911, and the husband called while the wife held onto Amore's reins. Cammie came back and grabbed Halla from me while I evaluated Sandy, who had regained consciousness. She was confused from her concussion and I didn't let her move her neck until the EMTs came and put her in spinal precautions. She went off in the ambulance, we walked the horses home, and then I went to the hospital.

Thankfully, Sandy only had a mild concussion, no fractures, and went home with a slight headache. Her helmet was cracked, and the doctors said chances were she'd have had a brain bleed, fractured skull or spinal chord injury without that helmet taking most of the impact.

This was the day that Amore began retirement, because after having her examined by the vet, it was discovered she had spinal arthritis, which was affecting her ability to support and balance a rider. Amore did not mind at all, and I began taking her for walks and ponying her behind Halla, which she seemed to enjoy.

Sometimes I ponder about how sometimes I was barely able to ride Halla using every ounce of my skill. What about horses that are even hotter than that; how do you ride them? I wonder sometimes about what leads to people breeding these horses into the world, and I wonder how most of the horses end up.

We had unusually hot weather on the weekend after Amore's accident, which meant everyone fled the city and came to the coast where it was about fifteen degrees cooler. On the beach there were paragliders going up and flying over our heads, umbrellas, tents, fires, dogs yapping everywhere, kids screaming, and remote control cars zipping around. We cantered Nala and Halla several miles down the beach, past many things. I briefly got off because a man was running a rather large remote control car and jumping it off ramps, and it must have been going forty mph. I didn't trust that he would be kind enough not to shoot it over toward our horses' legs and I thought I might not survive that.

The man acknowledged us with a wave and stopped his remote control car, so I hopped on and we cantered away. We made it to a little trail and Halla stepped into a hole I didn't see, while staring up at a man flying low in a parasail overhead. Halla stumbled precariously for about five feet before righting herself. I was sitting there riding it along and thinking, "No WAY! THIS horse is going down now, on the very next ride after Amore's fall?" But she didn't go down, and poor Nala behind us was trying to figure out what we were spooking at and what kind of spook that was.

At the end of the trail we spotted a little side trail that swooped up and disappeared. Nala's rider said, "I wonder where that goes?" Barely thinking about it, I steered Halla over and we hopped onto the trail. Unfortunately, at the crest the dune just dropped off steeply. It was only about ten feet down but Halla barely made it to the bottom upright. Nala was right behind us and there was no way to turn around. She scrambled over but is a bigger horse and it was even more difficult for her.

I hopped off and led Halla back up, turning her loose and catching her on the other side. I told Nala's rider I would catch Nala if she sent her over, but I barely did, catching a stirrup as she went by and yelling at her, which thankfully made her veer back so I could catch a rein.

After all that, when we walked back onto the beach it was simply packed with cars and people. There were low flying kites everywhere, and hordes of screaming kids. Halla began to work up, work up, and Nala's rider wanted to let her out. We cantered a little, but then I began to struggle with being unable to let out enough energy to go faster. Halla began just working sideways, up and down. It slowed us down a lot.

Finally we got past most of the mess and I tried for fifteen minutes to let some steam off Halla. Every time Nala got ahead, Halla began leaping and if I let her try to catch up she tried to put her head down and run. I corrected her several times, but she was beyond caring about that very much. Soon she began gathering herself up and hopping higher, and I could feel she was thinking about bucking me off. Unlike some horses, Halla knew exactly what she was capable of. Amore ditched me quite a few times on accident, but if Halla wanted to, I knew she could dump me on purpose.

Now we were passing someone folding one of the giant paragliders on the beach, and another one took off overhead. I told Nala's rider I was sorry but there was a naughty beast under me. We walked and trotted for a while, and I kept trying to manage Halla's energy. Finally, after a few minutes the beach cleared out some and I saw from Halla's neck and jaw that she had relaxed a slight amount. I tried to let her canter a little and finally she straightened up, began breathing and deflated some more. We ended the ride fairly calmly, and as always she had her head down and walked down the last bit to the barn as slowly as an old plow horse.

I decided to be careful not to ever get a hotter horse than Valhalla, because I think I went to the limit of my skill with her sometimes.

The next ride was just amazing. Cammie and I took Halla and Nala farther north on the beach than usual, went off onto a popular hiking trail and over three long wooden bridges, which the horses crossed very boldly. Then we went through a neighborhood, past a lake, back through a woodsy trail and then home via the beach. The ride had all types of obstacles and frightening objects, and we ended up going about nine miles.

When we first hit the beach we galloped the horses a solid one and a half miles, then cantered steadily for another mile. We took the trails slowly and then cantered back home about two miles when we hit the beach. The long gallop was the first time Halla had ended up "blowing" in the past few months, so we definitely added to the horses' fitness levels.

Now Satin needed some exercise so Rebel's owner, April agreed to ride her out with me on Halla and Cammie on Nala. Satin went very well in the Waterford bit, so it was good one of the horses was able to use it.

Unfortunately, it wasn't long before we had a little detour. We had cantered only about a quarter mile and the horses hadn't yet settled into a good gait when there was a large word written in the sand just in front of my path. Often I go around such things, because they can apparently appear 3D to horses and cause them to swerve. Today Halla looked at the word, and then I made the mistake of looking at it to read what it said.

"Kevin," I read, as Halla planted her right front foot, pulled up hard and leaped to the left. Finding myself off balance to the right on my saddle, I shoved my weight left. Unfortunately, Halla had followed my balance to the right so I basically threw myself off the saddle. It was a familiar feeling, leaving the saddle, so I turtled it and landed on my left side and back. Leaping up, I saw that Halla had run toward the dunes and was considering whether she should leave or stay.

I cajoled her very sweetly to please stay. She headed up the dunes and disappeared. I told my buddies that hopefully she was standing confused up top so they should stay down while I ran up after her. At the top, the grass was too tall and I couldn't even see a horse head above the waving grasses. I ran back to the top of the hill and motioned for Satin's rider to come up. Satin mistook the rider's signal and bolted up the hill, with Nala following close behind. I asked if they could see Halla from atop their horses, but they couldn't so I signaled for them to head back the way we'd come while I ran straight toward the posh neighborhood in front of us in case Halla had taken a straight line home.

I'm a runner, almost always in good enough shape to run for miles. But every time I've sprinted off after a disappearing horse I've noticed it is much harder to run in boots, half chaps, helmet and jeans, so I made it about a quarter mile before I was "blowing" myself. A helpful woman was weeding the spacious grounds outside her fancy house and saw me running,

"It ran that way!" I bolted off. A moment later, the woman came up behind me in her truck and asked if I wanted to hop in the bed. I hopped in and she drove me a block to where my friends were sitting on their horses, watching Halla a few dozen yards away. This time when I sweet-talked to Halla she stood still and let me gather her reins and hop back on.

So we thanked the nice lady and went out again.

This time I avoided the writing in the sand, and all went well. April had not been on such a long ride with us, and she said even though Satin was in shape, her own legs were shaking after the first long canter. When we came back around the point and let the horses loose, galloping a half mile, Satin's rider couldn't stop talking about how it felt, using words like "floating," and "magic," and "power." Words fall short...there are none to describe galloping full out on a horse. I think the best way to know about it is to look in the rider's eyes and you can see something there that goes deeper than words.

CHAPTER EIGHTEEN

Burning

You shouldn't wake up on the 4th of July with a song called "Burn it to the Ground" in your head. You might just think about taking your horse out for a ride on the beach. You might just feel an odd disconnection between what is probably wise and what is probably stupid, and not quite be able to figure out the difference. Then you might drink your coffee, focus on the equation again, and still find yourself unable to figure it out.

Finding myself in such a situation, I texted my friend, Cammie. Since I keep friends like her who gallop around on unstable Thoroughbreds, she could think of no reason why we shouldn't go down and "take a look." I also reasoned we could always come back and ride around the fields if the beach seemed too crazy.

We rode Halla and Nala down onto the beach in the early afternoon. To the south, we saw a virtual city of tents and cars so dense we couldn't tell where the gaps were in the distance. To the north; flags, tents, chairs, tarps, people claiming areas of beach as their own. We turned north.

After several minutes, Nala couldn't understand why we weren't running. There was so much stimulation but staring and staring at all the cars and flags and chairs was making her crazy. Our normally sparsely populated beach looked quite different today.

Close to the water we had some space to move. Nala was stretching her neck down and shaking her head, losing it a bit. Her rider began finding areas where she could let Nala take off at a fast canter for short stretches, and it began to calm her down.

Halla, on the other hand was not going to be able to stretch out. I found myself riding a fire-breathing dragon. Arabs have this odd talent of doing something I call "crazy legs." They can change normal gaits that are two beat or three beat and make them one beat, things like that.

We started doing a one beat canter down the beach. Normally, the three beats may be close together, but there's a one-two-three rhythm to it. Today Halla was hitting the ground with all four feet so closely to the same time that it felt just like one beat. She was also snorting with each stride so it sounded to me just like snort (airborne), snort (airborne). So we were going down the beach: snort-snort-snort-snort.

All the folks on the beach were in a festive mood and waved excitedly, beaming at us as we snort-snort-snorted by. Thankfully, the one beat canter requires TONS of energy and I could feel that while Nala was taking the steam off the top by running, Halla was working on a slow burn and it was helping keep her from boiling over.

To be honest, I know we would not have attempted such a thing with these horses a year prior, and we ended up very proud of them by the end of our ride. We passed by a hundred things that could have wrecked many horses. Halfway through the ride we took a break on our wooded trail away from the commotion, and the horses came right down from the emotional high and became calm. We steered through the maze of obstacles without any close calls for humans, dogs or horses.

After returning to the beach from the woods, Halla cantered normally and the horses looked and looked at everything as we passed by but did not spook, although I banged my stirrup against Nala's rider's stirrup about ten times when the horses called unscheduled safety huddles. I said we could probably enter in a parade, if it was one we could just canter through and wave as we passed by at high speed.

There's something within me that likes to take things right to the edge of what I could possibly be comfortable with, and to hang out there. Right where everything could go wrong, but I am pretty sure it's going to go right. Why that is, I'm not sure. I think perhaps it's because I'm a very mellow, mild, unexcitable person, and somehow I feel the need to push myself and not become stagnant. There were moments of discomfort on our ride, but also an underlying elation as we added to the horses' training, pushed out their comfort level a bit, and also pushed out our own.

Halla was working very solidly for me by now and her skills kept improving. She had figured out a few things.

One was that if I asked her to collect up at the canter, it would help her find the way through a rough patch of ground more easily. So she started gathering up very nicely for me when I asked.

Two was that she now understood my steering would help us neatly avoid obstacles in our path. Halla was the type of horse that had a natural resistance to things she didn't understand, and natural cooperation with things she did. So once she decided I had good steering and timing, and could judge our speed to help us avoid holes, logs, bumps and lumps, she responded very well to taking whatever path I chose for us.

Three is that she had learned that she was going to get to run and use her energy, and that she was going to get tired. So she began relaxing more and more and not worrying about whether she would gallop, and instead she would conserve her energy for the task at hand.

Such a smart horse; she also figured out that when we both saw a very smooth, flat piece of sand and I relaxed that I planned to let her stretch out. So I could feel in her body when she noticed that there was smooth sailing ahead, and the very instant I thought about letting her go, she was already beginning to stretch out.

I really enjoyed riding a horse with so many gears. Although I couldn't say she had gears at the trot, between her slow canter and fast gallop she had at least six gears. She was beginning to learn which gear I'd chosen at the moment, and would stay in that gear until I asked for a change.

My brave little horse was adapting so well, that one day we ran over some crab shells that crackled and it didn't startle Halla. We ran through a barrage of bubbles some children were blowing into the wind, and it didn't phase her or Nala.

A small child, about three years old sprinted away from his mother and began chasing us as fast as he could. The mother screamed, and ran after but could not catch him. Then she saw me laughing as I cantered on, because of course the child could never catch up fast enough to be in danger. She stopped running and began laughing too. I thought I probably just met either a one-day famous horse trainer or a one-day Olympic runner. He was determined to catch the horse, for sure.

After taking Halla out with Nala for a long ride, I met up with my friend, Sandy who was getting on Satin for the first time after her concussion. The doctor had cleared her for riding.

She confessed to me that she was nervous, and almost called me to cancel.

"Courage is being scared to death, and saddling up anyway." John Wayne.

Satin did not give her much time to think about that. She was up and prancy, and my friend had to keep her focused and busy. On the way home, she wanted to rush so my friend got off and made her walk on the lead so she went home at a slower pace. It was helpful that Halla was already tired, so set a good and calm example.

Another fine day when I ponied Amore down to the beach, she had not been down there since the accident, only around the fields so of course she had forgotten most of her courage. At first, she spooked at her shadow. If she caught sight of it in front of her, she stopped, leaned back and stared at it. When she turned her head for a better look, it moved and that was startling. On the way home, the wind was behind us and kept wrapping her tail around her legs. When her tail tangled around her legs, she kicked out and darted forward.

This happened about three times, and at first I couldn't figure out what was bothering her until April who was riding behind said it was her tail. HER TAIL. If you didn't believe me when I said she was the silliest horse there ever was, perhaps you do now.

When I brought her out around the fields the next day, she was trotting and looking back over her shoulder like something was chasing us, as if someone really had switched out her tail for a new one and she was having difficulty adjusting.

On the next nine mile ride with Halla and Nala, we decided to see how fast our horses were going. I had suspected Nala was very fast, based on how easily she left us behind versus other horses I'd ridden out with, and the last time we rode I wore my GPS watch so got some average speeds.

Halla's normal canter was about twelve to fourteen miles per hour and her trot about eight to nine miles per hour. Nala's trot was about fourteen miles per hour, and when Halla galloped it was around twenty-eight miles per hour. Nala was disappearing ahead of us so I figured she was probably going about ten miles per hour faster.

On this day I had Nala's rider wear the GPS watch so we could clock her. Nala's fast canter was around twenty-five miles per hour and her gallop went up to forty-seven miles per hour! Wow, we knew she was fast but that is very fast. The fastest sprint record I know of is fifty-five miles per hour.

Nala did not make it on the track, but I'm guessing as a three and four year old she wasn't mature enough mentally to settle since she was still "chucking riders off" at age ten when Cammie bought her. She was purchased as a dressage horse, but was too hot to handle ring work while living in a stall. Now at twelve years old and settling down, she was learning how to really gallop.

From what I've heard, Arabs gallop at speeds closer to thirty-five miles per hour. I'm guessing Halla was hitting thirty miles per hour sometimes and in her defense, she was twenty years old by now...I know we kept up with some Thoroughbreds that were slightly less speedy than Nala before Halla's knee injuries, and she still was a fairly swift horse.

Sometimes at my work it surprises people when an apparently passive one such as myself turns out to be a strong leader and they discover that some of the more obviously assertive types with their blustering do not provide someone to follow with confidence when things go south.

I believe this is why Halla was friends with me, and she could be a tricky horse to be friends with. She was a blusterer, strongly assertive, but did extremely well when we worked together rather than went head-to-head.

A typical conversation between us, both verbal and non-verbal:

"I am going to look at this scab, and put medicine on it."

"I could bite you if I wanted, see my teeth."

"OK, well I'm not going to harm you. If your leg comes off with the scab, feel free to bite my arm off."

"Fine, I'll stand still and watch but with that reservation."

Is that type of conversation acceptable with a horse? With Halla, I am not sure there was any other way. If you put a halter on, tied her up and forced her to stand while you treated her, the chances of you getting bitten or kicked would go up exponentially. If you left her loose, explained to her with voice and body language that you meant no harm, and left her the right to defend herself should her trust prove unfounded, you would come to no harm.

Trust with horses goes both ways. Why should they trust us if we don't trust them?

I'd been giving Halla some electrolytes with her vitamin E in a syringe because she didn't use her salt block and I worried about imbalances since she worked so hard. I tasted it myself and it makes your tongue want to turn inside out. I noticed Halla didn't like it, but she'd been very stoic about letting me syringe things into her mouth.

After I put it in her mouth, Halla was standing in her stall and some drool was coming out of her mouth as she waited for the bad taste to go away. As I sat watching her, she gave me this look I can only describe as pleading, and then she crept slowly over to me and pressed the flat of her forehead gently but firmly against my head, while still giving me this pathetic, wide-eyed begging look. What could I do? I told her no more electrolytes. I just had to trust that she would eat enough salt if she needed it.k3

CHAPTER NINETEEN

Firefighting

Halla was feeling really great. On one ride she was strong, powerful and moving well underneath me. I was trying out a new hackamore that had some leverage, but didn't seem too strong. We started off cantering with Nala, and it felt great with Halla going so balanced and straight. I'm in the habit of checking in every minute or two, to see how Halla's mental state is. Perhaps this is what the clinic instructors talk about...making sure the horse is "with you." But for me it's not about keeping the horse from spooking, but rather about making sure the horse hasn't decided to quit the team and start working on her own. Maybe that's the same thing for some horses...for my horses it wasn't: spooking was a fast, unthinking reaction that occurred whether Halla or Amore were totally with me mentally or totally not.

So I checked in with Halla - she didn't respond. Gave it another thirty seconds, checked in, no response. I should clarify...normally when we were working together, I'd give a little half halt with the reins, and feel a slight give in Halla's speed and position. She'd check her stride for a moment, and then I'd either then say "OK," and let her continue, or I would check her again and bring her back to whatever stride I wanted.

If what I was using was too weak, she would just take off and I'd have to turn her and use other measures to control the speed (and then not ride in it again). If what I was using was too strong, she would get upset and check back too hard, then her energy would start building and I would have to let some out. This combo was oddly exactly even: it wasn't strong enough for her to listen, but it wasn't weak enough for her to just take off either, so we got into this limbo where I was trying to check her speed but it didn't phase her. But I had enough strength to keep her from running faster. So it felt great to Halla, looked good on the outside, and yet we could have done a canter at a controlled (but fast) speed all day without me stopping my horse, until I told Nala's rider to slow down and then I was able to get a response from Halla.

I'd been in this limbo land with Halla before, a few times. It's not a bad place, it's just not one a person can regularly ride in because if something happens to change the equation (the horse finds extra power from excitement or fear), then you have a horse that is unable to get back with the team, and bad things can happen. Also my shoulders and lats would feel afterward like I'd been lifting weights or rowing a boat.

Nala's rider remarked on how happy Halla was about the whole situation. At one point Nala was confused because I had to turn Halla up a sand dune to help her slow, and Nala thought we were leaving the beach at an odd place.

I said that even in this case, Halla was not trying to dominate me; she was just trying to have more fun. Sometimes, I would be trying to stop her "fun," in a way, just because I was thinking bigger picture and about things we might run into if we went all out in the wrong place at the wrong time. She was not bad tempered; in fact she was quite good tempered to find out the opportunity that had come her way on this lovely day.

Well, I was always trying for something better for the horse, but it can't be too good for the horse and not quite good enough for the rider.

Thinking back, up until now I'd thought that when I first got Halla, we'd made tremendous progress, and then we had a backward turn for a while before this current progress again. When I really analyzed the past, I understood it differently. Our first couple of years we did make a lot of progress, but at first I treated her as a very green horse, and rode accordingly with horses and riders that made allowances for that. After that, I moved to a place where we rode trails that became predictable to us, and were almost always either alone, with Amore or another solid and mellow horse. It was progress, but also it was not so difficult for Halla to adjust to.

It wasn't until we moved to this barn where Halla ended up having health issues, that I thought we'd run into trouble and had to work on many things. The health issues did cause some problems, but what we also did was take things up to another level. Instead of riding with Amore or out alone, we now were riding with people who were on green horses or competitive horses, and some that did not make allowances for the person on the "hottest" or greenest horse.

Also, our environment changed from trails that were a minor variation on a theme, with tiny changes such as a flower blooming or a deer trotting by. Now we faced the wide-open and constantly changing landscape of the beach. Everything changed on the beach every day, from the location of the ocean, the texture and layout of the sand to what kind of debris is around and how many people, cars and kites are about.

It had been puzzling me a bit how I was able to ride in a kimberwicke for several years without finding it necessary to "tweak" things or make changes. At this point, changing bits in order to try to find the perfect communication tool, I saw it was because we'd actually progressed beyond where we were. We could now gallop around on wide open spaces with competition from not always completely controlled companions, and that was a whole new level of training. As a result, things needed fine-tuning. This was progress, and it was nice to see looking back that we'd actually come a long way from the first days of having other riders help us stop with their more solid minded horses, and being able to work Halla on my own.

I took Halla out with Nala in a mechanical hackamore for my next attempt at tweaking our communication. She was very compliant with it, and I was able to let her pace with Nala for probably three quarters of the ride or more. Often if I let her run with Nala instead of having her a bit behind and checking her pace, she would try to race. Then she would too excited and fight a little until I brought her back under control.

The result of Halla's compliance in the hackamore was a very fast ride. Both horses were extremely happy about it. For one thing, the sand was wonderful with a wide path near the ocean that was not so hard it felt like concrete, but still flat and hard enough that the horses didn't sink into it. There were very few people on the beach, and it was warm with a light breeze that cooled us off and dried the horses' sweat periodically.

At Nala's "racetrack," around the point, she took off and Halla was still compliant so I let her gallop out as long as she didn't stretch her head too low. We started out cantering past two older women who were standing agape with huge eyes, staring after Nala's speck disappearing into the distance. They turned as I approached, and I said, "We just let her go! She's a race horse so we catch up later." They were laughing and nodding, exclaiming about it. I doubt they'd ever seen a horse fly that close and fast before.

It didn't seem like Halla could really fight the hackamore. If she put her head too low, I'd give an intermittent pull on one rein to lift her a bit, and if she didn't do it right away I held the other side steady, which made the pull more forceful. None of this made her upset or made her try to push back, like some things we've tried. It was a very lovely ride.

The next day, Halla and I battled an elk.

We were going in a loop around the barn property, and were approaching the edge where several houses have yards that back up onto the big, open field where I was riding. Halla became very alert, and I guessed it was due to a new, large box that was sitting in one of the yards, similar to a large air conditioning unit.

Too late, I realized that she had smelled an elk that neither of us could see until it came charging out of the bushes at us.

It was a large female, and as she rushed at us I turned Halla to face her. I didn't know what else to do, and I hoped facing another large animal might give the elk some pause. The elk did stop, and backed up a step. I waited, hoping she would back off, but she held her ground. After a few moments, I tried turning Halla back to see if we could edge away.

As soon as Halla was not facing the elk, she charged again so I flipped Halla back around to face her. We tried this several times, and the elk was alarmingly close to where she could almost strike us with her hooves. Not knowing what else to do, I backed a couple of steps quickly to get out of range, hopped off and unclipped Halla's reins as fast as I could. I don't know how, exactly, but somehow Halla and I were a team and she rushed back several steps, turned to give me space, and then stood her ground while I whipped the reins around threateningly and hollered at the elk.

This finally made the elk spook off, back into the bushes. Halla was quite excited, but acted as though we had won a battle together. She came up, let me hook the reins back on and then I led her off for a ways to make sure we were far away from the elk before I got back on.

We always tried to give elk a wide berth, but I am guessing she was lying down and we surprised her. It was getting close to rutting season so the elk get edgy and more aggressive than usual. I was worried she was going to leap up and attack with her front legs while I was on the horse, and that did not seem like a good place to be. I think getting off made me more predator-like, and also the reins were something the elk did not understand and scared her.

After our elk incident, we went back to Amore's field and I ponied her behind Halla on another part of the property, far away from the female elk's territory.

CHAPTER TWENTY

Outings

Many people seem to really enjoy retirement, and Amore seemed to enjoy retirement as well. In her late twenties with Cushing's, and showing a few signs of slowing down a bit, she seemed to do fine with light, occasional exercise.

Amore was always fine with work, and capable physically of quite hard work. But I think she enjoyed her new role in life better. Perhaps it is the same sometimes for older folks who switch over into the retirement role.

Instead of work, Amore now went on "outings." As a result, she was quite happy to get out of the pasture for a change in routine, and go have some fun. I felt sorry when I would be in a rush to get a quick ride in with Halla, and Amore would spot me putting Halla's halter on from way out in the field. She would come running in, but we were already heading out without her.

It's understandable why she enjoyed her outings; usually they would go something like this: get an apple, get a halter on, go stand tied for ten minutes while getting all the itchy spots scratched. Go with Halla out walking for a mile, relax and see the scenery, stop and eat some nice grass. Go back to the barn, get a carrot, go back to the shelter and eat some nice hay.

One day I ponied Amore behind Halla down to the beach. This was the first time I had ponied a horse all the way down to the beach. I was either getting braver about ponying or more stupid.

It is much easier to pony a horse when the horse you're riding is in a leverage bit or hackamore. With the shanked hackamore, I was able to ride one handed and using just my pinkie finger I could apply enough pressure to direct rein through turns. I was also able to say with one hand, "Don't blast up the dune today, please walk," to Halla.

Of course, it is far easier to pony a horse in a western saddle, and in my dressage saddle I had to dedicate my right hand to holding the long lead I was using on Amore. There is nothing on a dressage saddle to dally around, so you just have to hold the entire rope.

I was reminded that I am not quite a good enough horseman to pony well, however. My poor horses. Halla stopped suddenly to pee at the top of the dune, and Amore didn't stop right away, got her head up even with Halla's, so I pulled back on her lead rope. Somehow I managed the timing just wrong and ended up knocking the two horses' heads together! There was a loud "thunk" as their skulls collided. Halla would have slaughtered another horse for doing that, but she is so indulgent toward Amore that she merely wrinkled her nose up and moved on.

As we rode, I remembered some of the reasons why I love fall on the Oregon coast. It was no longer hot, or bright, yet I was comfortable in a tee-shirt. People appreciate bright, and I can see why since it brings out the beautiful colors in the desert and makes the sky appear vastly blue. But coastal people get uncomfortable with brightness that lasts too long. We like grayness; the ability to open your eyes fully and stare at the world without sunglasses on.

In the fall, after several days of soaking, the sand on the beach loses all the treachery of the summer. In the summer, a fickle wind can arrange the sand lightly over deep holes and hidden pits. The reflection from the bright sun hides other hazards, and sometimes during a gallop we would take a serious stumble more than once. Having your life flash suddenly before your eyes gets old if it happens too often.

My husband and I came home after going away on a three-week vacation. There was a time when Halla, after three weeks off would be even more treacherous than summer sand. But on this day we had a beautiful ride. The mechanical hackamore still seemed to suit her fine.

Nala was a tiny bit tricky at first for her rider; although she had been ridden more in the past several weeks than Halla, she did have some time off for rainy weather as well. Halla just galloped over the reliable sand, and there was peace in my heart.

What a good gallop forces you to do is to live in the exact moment you're in, for a little while. You can't see far enough ahead to know how far you will go, if the footing will stay good, or if your horse will tire or need a bit of pulling back. But each stride is a moment, and you live it as it happens. It focuses a person, and it is everything you can do right then. Just ride, and be. I guess it's a form of meditation, or medication, for those of us who can't force our brains out of life so easily, and dislike drugs. No harmful side effects, as long as you don't fall off.

After riding Halla, she was sweaty and I didn't want to hose her now that she had quite a winter coat growing in. It was warm enough, probably mid-60s, so I used a brush and water bucket, which did not satisfy me as far as sweat removal goes, but she appreciated very much.

We were having a big storm. A cyclone off the coast was hopefully sweeping by and only giving us the remnants of the high winds on shore, with gusts around 70 mph. Higher winds can occur sometimes, if the cyclone comes in closer. But we'd also had quite a lot of rain coming down, and rain for several days.

Although the temperature was warm, I thought the horses might appreciate having their rain sheets on for the night. Here's how different my two horses were, although of similar age and the same breed.

When I brought the rain sheet into Amore's stall, she spooked and ran off into her runout. Then she stood with her eyes wildly bugging out, every muscle tensed as I fastened it on her. This horse had a blanket put on hundreds of times. Once the sheet was on, she relaxed a bit and went back to eating her hay.

Next, I brought the rain sheet into Halla's stall. She came rushing over, stood perfectly still and waited as I put it on her. Then she gave me this seriously reprimanding look, "What took you so long? It's been raining for days."

Amore was such an individual, and some would say there was "something wrong" with her brain. I've learned in the past few years that although we think of psychological problems in humans as relating to those who are literally in a state of psychosis, there is a continuum of how brains work that includes a wide range of what might be psychotic in an extreme, but can be also considered normal. Meaning, many people have tendencies toward paranoia without being psychotic. Many people have a tendency to be overly detail oriented, rule following and patterned without being obsessive compulsive to the point where they don't function well. People might have low mood or high mood, low energy or high energy without ranging into psychotic mania or depression.

I think horses are the same, and their brains are the same. We might not like dealing with all these varieties of personalities, but I feel a horse's personality is probably the most important factor we need to know when handling and training them.

Amore, although I considered her "normal," never retained memories of what was safe and what was unsafe very well. If she were a person, she'd be a very sweet but very neurotic lady who probably would take the bus instead of drive, would stay inside during storms, and would jump every time someone spoke to her out of the blue. What I did was take this neurotic little lady who would rather sit home in her apartment eating the same meal each day, and brought her to big sporting events and out hiking in the dark woods with wild animals around. Instead of being disappointed that my mare was still spooky in her late twenties, I was impressed with all the things she did that were so far removed from her nature. But I know she would always be a very spooky horse, no matter how many things I exposed her to. I am certain the wrong handling would have made her too neurotic to handle, but her training made her a horse that I could ride out in most situations.

Halla was more like someone who needed structure and rules. She really should have been in the military. Even with something like separation anxiety, the reasoning behind it is different for different horses. Halla was not afraid to be alone. She just wanted to know what the rules were. She also felt very responsible for other horses. So if I upset the normal routine and brought both horses down in the middle of the day to see the vet, she would get distressed. "I don't know what the rules are! Amore doesn't know what the rules are! How do I know if we're following the rules?"

If the vet were to come at 3 p.m. three days in a row, and the horses were put into a stall and given shots, Halla would have been a pro at it by the 3rd day. Amore would still have been confused.

If we always did something a certain way, Halla would become very solid with it. Unlike Amore, she only needed to be exposed to things a time or two before she understood they were not dangerous. With exposure, she grew very bold. She even carried other horses like Nala with her, showing them there was nothing to fear. Yet if you changed things so they were "not the way it is done," this upset Halla very much.

CHAPTER TWENTY-ONE

Weather

We went for an eight-mile ride with Cammie and Nala. The horses had not been ridden in a week due to inclement weather. When I say inclement, I mean my managers were calling to see if I was able to make it to work or would I need a ride? A tornado hit a town just south of us, trees fell down around us and some places flooded, typical winter weather, but it was still only fall.

We headed down the beach into a bracing headwind. The sustained winds were about thirty miles per hour. The sand was packed hard and if it were a racetrack it would have been described as fast. The horses had pent up energy. We let them out a little...or tried. Halla took off like a freight train. She certainly felt like riding a freight train; not a smooth, sleek bullet train but a rattling, banging, jolting back and forth freight train.

After flying about a mile, I asked Halla if we could slow down.

She said, "What?"

I asked again.

She said, "Did you say something?"

I asked again. Was she dishonest? Nah.

I don't know the right word to describe what she was. Self-possessed? Pompous? Something that was at once proud yet magnanimous but also self-protective. Her interests mattered and had to be respected.

She slowed down to a nice canter. The horses had gone so fast I had a hit of endorphins. My legs wobbled a little, not getting enough galloping in recently for legs of steel.

We went off the beach through the neighborhoods and sandy trail to get out of the wind for a bit. At the end of the trail near the estuary the winds were even stronger. Nala was pointing due west in front of us and her mane and tail were pointing due north.

Turning north, the wind was now strongly behind us. In the eight miles we saw six people on the beach, the die-hards. It was a glorious day to ride. Nala was burning. The changes in pressure from the storm, different routine, not enough exercise and too much standing out of the rain under her shelter all were built up inside. Her rider released the reins and she exploded forward. Normally she stretches out, long and extended. Today she looked so comical, but only Halla and I were there to see it and laugh. Her legs were trying to go faster than they could, and her gallop was a mad scramble of insanity.

Nala went one way around the giant bald eagle sitting on the knobby driftwood and Halla went the other. Halla was not insane with energy; she'd blasted it away during our first gallop. We settled into a lovely stride, and watched Nala disappear in several seconds. I am fairly sure with the tail wind and the very hard sand she beat all of her previous speed records.

It took us several minutes to catch Nala. She'd run extra far because her sign had blown down. There had been a sign about birds nesting in the dunes that Nala somehow decided months ago was her finish line, and always stopped running there. But the winds had torn it away so Nala didn't know where to stop. I'm guessing she decided it was time when Halla disappeared completely out of view behind her. Obviously Nala's rider had to wait for Nala to decide when the run was over, she was feeling that wild.

Nala was prone to such brief lapses of insanity that her mild snaffle seemed safe enough. Her intentions were much more labrador-like than Halla's.

The ride back home was controlled; the horses were quite sane, and I don't think either of them spooked once the whole ride. Halla still had extra energy at the end and was baiting Nala to take off by pretending she was going to trot off with her front legs and thrusting her neck forward. Nala was utterly calm and peaceful, so ignored the game.

I guess it was unicorns and rainbows after all.

Amore was very much herself for a couple of days.

The first day, I led her up to her pen and slipped her halter off. She was one step away from the open doorway, facing toward her hay net, it was dinnertime, and she was focused on the food. What would go wrong? I did this sometimes, let the horse go when they were right at the open gate since they knew the routine of heading in to eat. Halla and Rebel were already in their pens. Same old routine.

A slight sound as Amore stepped forward caused her to veer of course by one inch, which somehow allowed her to miss her doorway and head around the side of the barn. Bright green grass caught her eye, so she stopped to graze.

"Amore," I said. This startled her, so she lifted her head, saw a goat and ran off around the other side of the barn. Fine, I was sure she'd think about her hay and head back to her pen.

I walked around the edge but didn't see her. I looked in the barn but didn't see her in the aisle way.

"She went in the barn," my fellow boarder told me. I went in and found Amore in the back, in an empty stall. A couple years ago she had been put in this stall at night for a couple months. She was in there looking very lost and confused. There was no food in there for her.

After leading Amore back to her pen, she ran in and found her hay net. She was especially pleased about being in her own stall after having been so lost.

The next day, I had both horses out grazing. I set down the lead ropes as I sometimes do, knowing the horses were occupied. Glancing up, I saw Amore step on her lead. Suddenly, all of her body parts flew in multiple directions except she managed to keep the one leg in place that was standing on her lead. The clip broke, lead rope fell off, Amore stood for a second, "Oh!" and then went back to grazing. Halla did not react. Every horse that has been around Amore for more than a few days stops reacting to what she does. They soon figure out she is an odd one.

It started raining so I moved the horses into the aisle way of the barn. I tied Amore outside a stall that had an open doorway. Two feet of lead loose, a bucket securely on a chest nearby...I thought about the bucket and the open doorway, but didn't think Amore could get into too much trouble on a short tie.

Began working on Halla's hooves. Bang! The bucket rattled away. Amore spooked backward around the corner so her butt was inside the stall and her head out. She was stuck there, unable to figure out how to move and get back out of the stall since her lead was now taut. She stood there as though tied that way, looking very confused. I kept trimming. Halla never blinked.

A couple minutes later, a horse in the barn rustled. Amore spooked and fell down the two inch step that went into the stall, stumbled and then ended up standing nearly where she'd started with her tail flipped around up over her back. She still looked confused. I was done trimming by now, so gave the horses each a carrot and put them into their pens for the night.

One afternoon it was quite mystical on the beach. I am not sure where the word comes from, but I understand "mistical" since we have so much fog and mist here. Things look surreal and the light shimmers a bit oddly, almost as if you were in a fairy tale (or horror tale, depending on your fancy).

Many of us in Oregon consider fog as dense and something you can see visibly floating. Mist is more of a veil that changes the vision, and misting is something that can be felt on the skin. Today there was mist, but only right near the ocean so when Cammie and I went out, we passed from full sun at the barn quickly into another, hazier world.

Surprise! When we got to the top of the dunes, the ocean was in very close and the sand was mostly covered with foam. What sand we had available was bumpy and not good for galloping. With uncertainty, we wandered out to see how the ride would go.

There was very little wind. The foam was piled up high, in some places as high as the horses' knees and sometimes crossing nearly the entire beach.

We soon discovered we could safely canter. There was very little wind to send chunks of foam chasing after us. At first it was like an obstacle course. There were huge piles of the octopus-like seaweed that washes up on the beach. The horses quickly remembered what foam was and that it did not hurt horses. Soon they were plowing right through it.

It was interesting to us how one piece of seaweed alone on a bare beach was something the horses would view with caution, but if a beach was covered with seaweed, they ignored it.

It seemed good to me that we had a ride where the horses were fresh and wanted to gallop, we were not able to let them gallop, and they didn't get too hot about it. Halla did request a gallop, more than several times, but responded well when I told her we could not because the sand was too bumpy.

We ended up going on several trails off beach, and went north farther than we'd gone before. There was a very long wooden bridge and it was not exactly safe to cross because the horses slipped several times, but only one hoof went out at a time so we made it fine.

When we hit the beach again and began cantering, I felt Halla get very bold. It was like she was scoffing at the foam. "It doesn't hurt horses!" She started aiming for some of it and stomping along through.

Nala was now wanting a gallop badly, so her rider let her go for a very short one. I kept Halla mainly cantering because I couldn't remember where the sand turned bumpy. The ocean had drifted out a bit so we had more room, and it had taken some of the foam with it.

We went over a couple of logs and Nala went over one I thought looked a bit large, but Nala's rider couldn't see the other side with a drop that I did. Halfway over, Nala stretched out to clear the drop and it was a nice big jump.

Nala picked up a working trot and Halla did a lovely slow canter, finally relaxing nicely. The last mile and a half home we cooled the horses out and they came in quite pleased with themselves, a bit tired, and thinking of dinner.

CHAPTER TWENTY-TWO

Lessons

Horses are the best teachers, if we're willing to learn. Not just horse lessons, but life lessons as well. Halla was a horse that tested, that took advantage, that looked for signs of weakness. She was this strange combination of insecurity and boldness. In a way, we were direct opposites. She was bold and bossy until something made her lose courage. I am passive, do not insist, and am not so bold until something forces me to rise to the occasion. Halla made me rise.

Potentially, a horse so assertive could run all over a person who was passive. Yet that horse taught me: act, or I will. Insist, or I will take over. If you don't lead, I will. In many ways, Halla was a horse that elevated me as a rider, a horse that insisted I step up and lead or she would become the boss. She was sharp, she was difficult, extremely opinionated and perfect.

Something I learned about the hackamore and about both my horses that could be sharp: you're never going to hit the nail exactly on the head when it comes to the right level of bridling. It seems to me with the sharper horses, it is far better to err on the side of too soft rather than too harsh. With Halla, the margin of safety with too soft was not very wide. I couldn't just put her in something that she didn't feel, or she would take over the world.

The English hackamore worked well and she was extremely happy with it. If I let her gallop full out, it would take us a bit of time to slow and stop. With a curb bit, that was something I could do quickly if necessary. Yet I was comfortable with this margin because my horse was safe enough, yet happy.

Halla was my litmus test of how severe things were. Those who say an English hackamore is harsh have not ridden a strong horse in one. Halla would tolerate quite a lot of pressure from the hackamore, which she would not do with the curb bit. When I palpated around her head and looked for rubs, sore areas, or pulled hair she never seemed to have any. There was some pressure, because she did have incentive to listen to me. Without that she would have taken full advantage. But it was not much more than an "ask," for sure. It was something that for her could be ridden with a constant feel, without her shaking her head or being bothered by it. That was something I'd never heard about this device, that even with leverage a nose squeeze is dull and not sharp.

Here's how Halla was: One time I rode, I went in the treeless saddle which I hadn't ridden in for some time. With the hackamore rather than the curb, I definitely did not have a solid base of support for leverage and Halla took full advantage. I could not let her full out, because at even halfway out she was gleefully taking over the job of "boss" and telling me what we were going to do rather than listening to my ideas.

The next time, I had the dressage saddle on, but I'd changed out the stirrup leathers. Even though I measured three times against the old ones, they still ended up too short. There is this sweet spot with stirrups and depending on the horse, it can make a huge difference. We started galloping and I was too high, without enough leg for ballast. Having had free rein the last time we rode, Halla tanked off and ignored my attempts at conversation. When she put her head down at the gallop, if my core was too high it meant the reins were very long and she had tons of leverage.

After a couple miles, I hopped off and fixed my stirrups. Halla tested, stretched out, and we cantered off with me having the balance of power now skewed in my favor. She did several stretched out leaps, almost small bucks but too extended to matter. Then she settled right into communicating with me again. Now my opinion was given a bit of weight, and now we were headed back toward a 50/50 partnership.

Did I take this personally? Did I think if I had a better relationship with my horse she wouldn't be this way? I'm not sure why I would. Halla had two good friends and I could see she cared for them very much. Amore and Nala were her great buddies and Halla showed great concern for Amore, watching over her well being in the field, protecting her from horses over the fence, letting her in the shelter when it rained, keeping horses from running her off the water trough. Yet she also ruled over Amore and Nala, pushed them around, asserted her will and enforced her rules.

In a way, I think she was insecure about having no one in charge, and this meant she had to test and see and know who was calling the shots each day. I had to keep proving my own position with her, and when I did I believe she was happier for it. Even if it meant she couldn't gallop freely and uninhibited at whatever speed she liked.

We had a very fun time on the trails one day, with Halla and Nala trotting out. It was like a video game and quite challenging. I had to watch for branches overhead, for knee knockers on both sides, for holes and unevenness in the ground at our feet. Meanwhile, I had to look ahead, note the angles of the curves, and thread my horse through the eye of the needle between trees. All the while keeping my horse to a trot as she insisted we could probably do it all at a canter.

People can think that if a horse takes over or takes off, there is something wrong with the friendship. Why would a friend want to do this? I don't think a horse finds the harm in this that we might. They don't think about our desire to avoid potholes or to keep the speed down to our level of comfort. Halla was not in a power struggle with me emotionally, she just had a mind that worked out the puzzles and discovered if she could be the one calling the shots. It seemed impersonal, like someone beating you in a chess game. I've known one other horse that was like this, playing chess with you. But he was a gelding and only played on occasion, rather than on every ride. Oh the joy of mares.

It always rains here in the winter, but there are frequent breaks where you can slip out between showers. This particular November the breaks were too short and infrequent, and Thanksgiving day it was the rainiest place in the U.S. with 4.4 inches of rain.

We had a day where it did not rain for our entire ride, and the horses enjoyed their gallops to the extreme. Poor Nala needed her gallops and was a little beside herself until she got it out of her system. She kept looking for something to spook at, but nothing appeared! I adore thoroughbreds but they are slightly less creative than Arabs, I must say.

Another time I arrived for our ride ten minutes late, when I pulled in I found Nala saddled and her rider ready to go. I'd seen driving in that my horses were waaaay out at the far end of the pasture, so I jogged all the way up the hill and through the gates, not wanting Cammie to have to wait long for me.

Grabbing Halla's halter, I began jogging down the hill into the field. This unexpected sight of me running toward them flummoxed the horses. They galloped in straightaway, tails flying, with Amore looking very perturbed. Once they hit the top of the hill where I was, they stopped suddenly and looked surprised.

"Oh, carrots, thanks." I haltered Halla and Amore stared around wildly for a minute or two before diving down to eat some grass and then casually saunter away.

Sometimes going outside here in the winter is very gloomy. Although I was at the barn by one on an early afternoon, it was gray as dusk and the skies were glowering. As with most places, there is a time of year on our coast where the weather is less than ideal for outdoor activity. December and January here are the two months where the sun is completely hidden even on the best days, the sky is never blue, and every view of the outdoors would make an appropriate background for a ghost story.

"It was a dark and stormy...day."

I do appreciate that our temperatures stay above freezing 99% of the time, and understand that what we think of as a warm jacket is more like a light, inner layer in some climates.

Nala's rider did not respond to my text, so I saddled up Halla to take her out for a ride alone. It was not raining. Therefore, the weather was quite fine. The wind was steady without large gusts.

The beach was only about forty feet wide. More than half of that was littered with debris, leaving only about ten feet of usable sand; a narrow strip that ran along the pounding waves. The ocean roared and spit foam at us. It had been some time since Halla had gone out to the beach alone.

We did a very collected canter for a mile down the beach. It was collected enough that Halla was able to shorten her stride and neatly fit between and around all the piles of seaweed, broken branches, large drift logs and the occasional plastic lid or soda pop can that all mixed together in the sand. In my mind we were doing a version of working equitation like the Spanish horses do. We had the power, the lift and control to safely maneuver around all the flotsam that could have tripped a horse or made her stumble.

Halla was an amazing horse. The waves were fourteen feet high and some of the foam balls that came rolling toward us were as large as basketballs. She avoided some things, such as the surf surges that came in too far unexpectedly and some of the foam pieces that seemed large and unpredictable. But she never spooked at one thing. Smaller bits of foam hit her legs and she kept going without flinching.

After a mile, I realized the tide was coming in even further, and our ten foot strip was under water. It was time to turn around. We couldn't quite avoid all the debris now, as there was not always a pathway around it, so we had to intersperse some trotting between our canter strides for safety. Halla was fine with it because she saw the necessity. She preferred not to trot if she could canter, but if there was a good reason to actually trot, she would.

Once we got back to the field near the barn, Halla got a bit snorty and wouldn't settle into a calm walk. I let her prance for awhile before asking her to slow, and then continued up the hill to gather Amore and take her out for a short pony ride. Halla appreciated having Amore come along, and began to cool down nicely. I stopped to get off and let both horses graze for a while, and they were pleased to find some taller grass that had not been cropped short like the grass in their pasture.

I realized that I often would just take my horses out when they were planning to go in and have dinner, and tie them for a bit, or take them out to the arena. I expected them to do what I asked, regardless.

When I say "expected," it doesn't imply I forced any manners on them. They were just resigned, knowing that my stubbornness and strength of will were too strong for them. It did no good to fuss or protest, because even if they were to go away from the barn bucking and snorting, I'd still drag them up to the arena and ride. After a time, horses just give up on people who are so persistent. Punishment can turn into something interesting, or a game. Stubbornness is much more difficult to resist, like a tidal wave it just keeps coming and there's nothing a poor horse can do to combat it.

CHAPTER TWENTY-THREE

Manners

Halla was feeling extremely superior to Nala on this day. She just exuded disdain, especially because Nala had not been out for a gallop since the last ride we'd done together (Halla has been out twice since then) and she was feeling very edgy. Nala kept bursting forward into a trot, and her rider circled her back. This was on the half mile warm up walk we always did down to the beach. Halla walked extra slowly, looking away as if she couldn't be bothered to notice what Nala was doing. It was all a show. Now mind you, Halla would often take Nala's cues and trot to catch up when we went toward the beach. Today she was saying that no matter what Nala did, she was going to do her own thing.

I had a new saddle on Halla, and it felt nice, the stirrup bar placement quite ideal.

We got to the beach and Halla continued sauntering along at a walk. Finally I tired of the game, so asked her to trot and then canter. Both horses showed their true colors and the pent up energy we knew was in there had to come out. Halla galloped a bit madly for a while.

We continued at different paces, sometimes getting drenched by the rain. It was great to have my gloves and rubber reins. No concerns about the reins slipping out of my grasp if I didn't pay attention.

One of the boarders at the barn who owned a mustang was the one who most often brought my horses in to their pens at night. Amore liked to get to her food quickly, so when you took her halter off she would wait until it started to drop, then she'd duck her nose out and trot off towards her hay. I didn't find this particularly rude or annoying, so I let her do it. One night when Amore came down the hill, I saw that the mustang's owner had Amore turn away from her food and stand quietly waiting while her halter was taken off. Then she turned slowly and walked to her food. She told me she had taught Amore this in two times trying it, because she just didn't care for the excited frame of mind and wanted her to be calm. I thought it was cute, and I thanked her nicely, saying I appreciated it.

I didn't mention that Amore had been trained to do this - well, who knows how many times before. It all depended on what the person handling her wanted. I also didn't mention that there would be days when Amore came in crazy eyed, and she wasn't going to be capable of standing quietly or walking to her food. Amore knew many things, and if you did your part, sometimes she would do hers. You just shouldn't count on it.

One of the joys of winter was doing the horses' hoof trimming by the light of a headlamp. Halla played this little game where she lifted one back hoof just slightly as I was trimming the opposite front. It wasn't enough to where I could let go of the front and make her lose her balance - when I tried that she just shifted her weight slightly back onto the lifted leg. But each time I'd get to working, she'd lean just that bit to where I was taking an uncomfortable amount of her weight. I could tell it amused her very much. She loved playing games, seeing what she could get away with. I guess she knew when her games were harmless enough, if my objections were weak and I kept laughing between protests.

I guess some people think if you let horses get away with these poor manners, they will get worse and worse until the horse is a bad citizen. It didn't seem like that to me. Nala wasn't going to start pulling back and destroying her halters because she liked to untie herself once in awhile and wander away. Halla wasn't going to start smashing me under her body weight or kicking during hoof trimming. These were games, the kind horses play.

Nala's rider, Cammie met someone through a local riding group who wanted to meet up at the beach. Knowing nothing about this person, I decided to put the curb bit on Halla in case the new horse needed someone to stay back while Nala went running off.

I had a new fleece saddle cover on for the first time (Christmas present) and it was very comfortable. It didn't slip around at all. My stirrups felt a bit longer suddenly due to the lift, and I asked Nala's rider if she thought it would squash down after a bit. She said it might take awhile since I didn't sit down very much!

The rider texted to say she was waiting in the parking lot at the beach entrance. Due to their discussions previously, Cammie thought this was the parking lot one mile south on the beach. At the parking lot there was a horse trailer but no rider. Cammie said she recognized the trailer as belonging to another friend she'd ridden with several times before, someone who was currently training a Friesian.

We discovered the other rider was waiting for us at the next parking lot north, now about four miles away. We told the rider to head south and we'd head north and meet up. As we left, we saw the Friesian with her rider, about a half-mile south. There were a couple people walking alongside, because the trainer was demonstrating to the owner how the horse was coming along.

Cammie said the Friesian had recently cantered for the first time, alongside Nala, but had only been excited at the trot, not wanting to run off with Nala whatsoever. This was Nala's third or fourth ride of the week, so she was feeling fairly angelic. Cammie said they had gone to an arena, where she'd had a different horse than she was used to. In the arena Nala was super light, responded immediately to cues and had progressed quite a lot since the last time she'd been ridden in an arena.

I've learned this, that if a horse can respond to the fast pace and difficult terrain outdoors, they improve dramatically for arena riding. They get fit enough to carry themselves in that smaller area more easily too. I'm really beginning to feel the best way to train a horse is teach the first basics in the arena, then take them outdoors and ride all over the place. It teaches them what you want them to know much better than drilling in the arena.

We thought we'd better wear out the horses a bit, so cantered north. After about two and a half miles we saw the other rider cantering toward us. Here came a cute little Arab, and a nice retired lady who used to do endurance and was thinking about doing it again. She liked doing cowboy dressage with her gelding, had another Arab she said was "hotter" and might do better if she did endurance again. She thought looking at us that we were endurance riders. She seemed to like our horses and said she hadn't seen horses that muscled up in a long time.

We had a great time. Halla was worked up at first, and popped her butt up at Nala once we got onto our narrow wooded trail. She seemed to want the new gelding to notice her and pranced her very best to show how beautiful she was. She also wanted him to know she was the one in charge.

Once we got back to the beach, we trotted and cantered a bit, and the new rider said she could tell our horses had endurance minds. Halla tried to dart past the new gelding to see if he would race, but he maintained a steady canter. Later they trotted head to head, and Halla went like that for about a quarter mile even though she usually didn't like to sustain a trot. Their paces were matched evenly, and little Arab had a beautiful floating trot.

We ended up going about ten miles, and we had very well behaved horses after we bid goodbye to the woman and her Arab.

CHAPTER TWENTY-FOUR

Laminitis

Halla had a nagging lameness show up. It seemed like she was favoring a hind leg, but it was difficult to figure out what was bothering her for several days. When it didn't clear up, I had the vet out to see her. The vet watched Halla moving for a while, and was unsure about what the problem was. Finally she took some hoof testers out and pressed them together on the soles of Halla's front hooves. Halla went straight up, rearing away from the pressure.

Laminitis! It was something I hadn't worried about with Halla, since she'd always had sturdy, sound little hooves and it was difficult to keep weight on rather than a struggle to keep her thin. I'd worried about it with Amore, since she tended to gain weight easily.

Over the next week, the pain in Halla's hooves got worse. She was taken off all grass, her oats, and put on a low sugar/starch hay and hay pellets. Her hoof x-rays showed a little rotation of the coffin bone, but her tests for Cushing's disease or Insulin Resistance came up negative. That was all good news, and I was hopeful that my mare would soon recover and we'd be out riding again in several months. She was getting an anti-inflammatory so I gave her a medication to prevent ulcers.

Cammie was sympathetic about Halla's condition, and also felt sorry for me since one of my horses was retired and the other recovering from laminitis. She offered to let me ride Nala whenever I wished.

One afternoon I took Nala out for a ride. The first trick was to saddle her, bridle her and get the stirrups adjusted to my height. Cammie had some magical trick of timing where she swooped up the saddle, pad and got the girth tightened in a couple quick motions. Well, she was quite a bit taller than me. I kept trying to readjust things, and Nala was nodding her head and swinging back and forth, saying hurry up, hurry up. Finally I got on and rode up to the field. Then Nala realized it was almost dinnertime, turning into dusk, she was alone, and what had happened to the bottom half of my legs? Her owner is quite a bit taller and weighs a bit more than I do. She was wondering why someone had put a jockey back on her...weren't her racetrack days over?

Nala turned back toward home twice, and I pointed her back where we were going, and then had her trot to ease her mind. She didn't really respond to my legs, just my seat. Too short. There was some major roofing going on as we walked through the neighborhood, and some ships were in close on the ocean with strange lights that Nala stopped and stared at. I got off and walked her past everything, onto the dunes because her head was high and she felt tense.

Once on the beach, Nala felt better. I got on and we long trotted a while, and then cantered. A small part of my mind thought about letting her gallop. But the larger, smarter part of my brain knew that would not be wise. I had limited time, who knows how far we'd go, it was dusk, there were bonfires, I was alone, no one had ridden Nala besides her owner in about a year (when I last rode her) and it would take a little more time to work together as a team with this horse.

Nala was very smooth and very balanced. I'd been riding just Halla too much lately, so I had to remember not to over steer. Because Nala was so balanced, I could shift her off a straight line without meaning to, and I kept over steering. Halla was not built anywhere near symmetrical to begin with and then damaged her knees and also suffered muscle damage from her vitamin E deficiency. Besides being crooked, her range of motion in the front legs was decreased. It almost felt like Halla had to lift herself up across her own centerline to change direction. She was very athletic and compensated. But compensation did not feel anything like a well-built, athletic horse that had never been injured and was super fit.

So long trotting down the beach, Nala adjusted her line of travel six times in a row to just a few inches left, just a few inches right, and back and forth. Finally I put my reins down on her neck and bridged them, and settled my line of sight out farther so she wouldn't think a drunken jockey was riding her. She was trying very hard to accommodate my unintended requests. But now we went straight, and if I wanted to make a circle I used both reins, gradually, together, and that helped us not veer so sharply.

Her canter was so smooth, and covered so much ground; it just felt like I was barely moving until I noticed that I was going very far and very fast. It must have been only three minutes before we had gone the mile down to the next beach access. If I'd thought her gallop was similar, I would have tried it out despite my good safety logic, but her owner reported it was a bit rough and sometimes she had to hold mane.

124

Once we got back up the dune and past the loud construction, Nala walked home very calmly on a loose rein. I knew I hadn't done much to help exercise Nala compared to her usual workouts, but thought at least this little outlet might have taken some of the mental energy off her.

When I see energy in my horses, bursting out of them, I think positively. I think I am seeing signs of good health. I think I am seeing energy to be ridden and to burn off with work. When I see calmness, I think that is good too, in the right setting. But when I was working on things and my horses were not very calm, that was fine because I could channel their energy positively and get them focused on things that were difficult, and that they would need the energy for.

My friend wanted Amore to approach her food calmly. That was great. But if she ever approached her food so calmly she was indifferent, I would worry. I was actually more happy to see her having interest in food and life and energy to do things. That is something I value more than calmness, myself.

Amore was bonkers one day. I mean totally nuts.

I put the horses out in a small field temporarily in the late afternoon while I cleaned their stalls and pens. This field was close to the creek, and apparently some flies were buzzing around. Amore had sweet itch, so was particularly sensitive to midges.

When I was done cleaning stalls, I went into the goat pen and trimmed the goat hooves. I kept hearing loud snorts and pounding noises, so finished quickly and went to check on the horses.

Amore looked like she'd burrowed underground somehow, with muck all over, even covering her ears. The horses were galloping around, which wasn't good since that field was supposed to be resting and growing. So I quickly pulled the horses out and tied them, planning to trim Amore's hooves.

Amore was trying to scratch her stomach by throwing both hind hooves forward at once underneath it. I squelched some of the muck off and scratched her belly really well with a long bristled brush, then put fly spray on her.

As I trimmed her front hooves, Amore continued flinging one hind hoof up and out. I warned her a couple times. She did try flinging both hind hooves while standing on just one front (since I was trimming the other), but I told her that wasn't acceptable.

125

She stopped temporarily while I trimmed the hinds, but the second I finished she threw a hind up to the side higher than her own flank and caught me with it.

She'd been thinking that flies were the most important things in the world. Suddenly she realized flies were NOT the most important thing, as we locked eyes. Hers nearly popped out of her head and she backed to the end of her lead as I explained clearly to her that she had made a bad mistake.

Halla stood next to Amore, so smugly. It was time to trim her hind hooves, since I'd only done her front hooves last week. Her hinds looked quite perfect, with no apparent effects from the laminitis.

She rarely ever stood perfectly to have her hinds trimmed without pulling away once, but I swear it was making her feel superior to be well behaved when Amore was in trouble. She picked up each hoof before I asked, planted it into my hands and even held up all her weight without leaning while I filed. She looked over at Amore with her nose in the air.

CHAPTER TWENTY-FIVE

Fine Lines

Halla was recovered enough by now to try some light riding. I thought to make things easy for Halla by putting Amore in the outdoor arena while we rode around the field. However, Amore took off the moment I let her loose, as if a coyote was hanging onto her tail. She bolted around, crashing over the jump blocks that had been set out in the ring and snorting loudly.

I got on Halla and we started walking, but she spooked a couple times at Amore. She was behaving so crazy it was like she was going to leap over the railing on top of us or something.

I took Halla away, far across the field. Of course, once we were off on our own, Amore's crazy antics began to make sense to Halla. Maybe she was right - maybe she knew about some danger out here.

Halla did a couple little galumphs and kafuffles and skitters sideways. Then she took a good look at Amore, decided she was nuts and then we walked calmly around for a few minutes.

We went back and walked around the outer border of the arena, at which point Amore finally settled and started grazing.

Halla moved well and it was a nice, short little ride.

Afterward I had to spend quite a long time raking over the giant craters and skid marks Amore had put in the arena. We're supposed to leave it nice for the next person, and it looked like someone had turned a herd of buffalo loose in there.

Amore didn't harm herself or even turn a hair, and appeared quite calm eating her hay when I left. Silly horse.

Halla reacts to odors very strongly. One day I put fly spray on Amore in her stall. Several minutes after I sprayed Amore, the smell of the spray must have wafted over into Halla's stall. I thought Halla was colicking or going to have a seizure. She started acting so strangely, put her head between her front legs, then her ears and lips started twitching. She kept pawing like she was going to roll, and then she'd stop. Finally I realized it was that smell, and once it blew away on the wind she was normal again.

Although I was still taking things very easy with Halla, by this time I was very pleased with how her hooves were doing. So far there were no signs of soreness from our little rides. Down to the beach was about a half mile, so I decided to go down and back, riding Halla and ponying Amore for around a mile, would be was the farthest we'd gone so far since the laminitis.

On this particular summer day, the horses were abnormally calm from the heat. Poor Amore had signs of dried sweat on her coat. Although she was shedding out better this year than the previous year, due to increasing her Prascend dose for her Cushing's, she still had a medium coat left. Today was a little too warm for what she was still wearing.

The mares walked very calmly all the way to the beach, with Amore only trying for a bite of grass a couple times. I was watching for that, so I caught her before she could get her head down and plant herself. We even passed by three little deer that bolted up a hill, and the horses just watched them go.

Once we caught sight of the ocean and turned back for home (we didn't go down the dunes), Halla got a little excited. I think she was planning to go down and run on the beach, so got a little hit of adrenaline. After prancing along for a little bit, she started plunging every couple of strides. If you don't know what plunging is, it's kind of like what horses do when going through deep water. It feels like the horse is thinking about bucking or cantering, but they don't quite launch.

I wasn't sure if I could keep a hold on Amore's lead if Halla kept plunging, so I got off and walked the horses for a little bit, stopping to let them graze. Halla had some shaky legs going on, I noticed, so I guess it was a little too exciting for her to be back out near the beach again.

She was wearing her Renegade boots, so we were able to go across the asphalt and gravel road with no worries. Once we were back in the field near the barn, I got on and ponied Amore again. Halla plunged a couple more times, but it was not a concern since Amore could safely get loose within the fenced area, and I knew she'd just start grazing if she did. Halla didn't really do anything rough, just thought about it.

Amore stayed calm throughout, only getting excited when her nose got too close to tall grass.

By now I was remembering what it was like to get Halla back into working again. This was the fifth time or so I'd done it, and it was always quite a crazy thing. The two times that were most involved up to this point were when she had her knee injuries, and after her Vitamin E deficiency.

There was this tenuous period of time where Halla started feeling great, and the energy was bursting out of her body. Getting this horse into shape was quite tricky. There was this nice, safe period where she was very out of shape and content to walk along and do a little jogging. There was also the final outcome where she had gained enough fitness to where I felt safe to let her canter for some distance or gallop and let her energy burn off.

Between the two would come a between time which was what we were getting into now, and that was a time that required a lot of skill and caution. I had to manage her energy safely, without letting her run off too soon and harm herself. But she was not a horse that was good at doing a moderate pace without ever going fast. Keeping her speed and energy contained was very tough.

On this day we went along a little trail and then around one of the big fields. When she was like this, applying pressure to the rein was like you were holding down the volume up button for a TV. The longer you hold it, the louder it gets, and when you held the rein her pressure would go up that fast.

When she was fit, Halla would tolerate even constant pressure on the bit. She would work into and through it. When she was in this in between state of too much energy that I couldn't just run off of her, I had to keep a looser rein and apply the aids very judiciously.

There was no chance we were just walking this day, so I tried to let the energy out with short periods of trotting and tried to keep any canter down to three strides. Halla knew I was going to hold her speed back, so when she cantered she'd burst into it, and leap very high for a couple strides. But when I touched the rein she'd come right out of it.

I didn't want her to fall into any of the bad crookedness habits she learned after her Vitamin E deficiency. She didn't currently have that kind of muscle wasting, so I didn't think it would be an issue. I directed her energy sideways several times when she wanted to progress rapidly forward toward rough ground I wanted to miss, and she stayed straight through her body or followed the bend I asked for so that was good. Yeesh, with her even a short ride could turn into a workout.

People often ask about how to "shut down" a horse. If you rode Halla you'd understand how dangerous thinking that way could be with some horses. You could easily feel when riding her that any attempt to shut down the energy was going to push the volume button up up up until the horse exploded and left you in a pile on the ground.

You could not shut her down; instead, you would have to manage her energy. Let it out, let her go a few steps, and then gather her back in. When the energy started to rise, do that again. It was interesting how this would gradually bring the energy back down until she was walking calmly again, but trying to stop her or keep her speed too slow initially would ramp up her energy until it was out of control.

She was just that kind of horse, even now at age twenty-one. But I knew that once I had her running on the beach a couple times a week again, she would become a lot more docile. Nala was the same, a hotblood for sure. They will get more mellow if totally out of work and not being asked to do a thing. They will also be mellow if they are in hard work. But they don't tolerate working lightly. It's not in their nature.

One night I felt a little "high."

I rode Halla on the beach for the first time since her laminitis. We went with Nala, and Cammie was willing to go for a short distance and slow, so we wouldn't let Halla do more than she might be able to handle.

Some people believe that no horse enjoys being ridden. If I'd only ever ridden Amore, I might have thought that. She didn't obviously show joy when ridden, and seemed rather to tolerate it.

But I've been on many horses that enjoy going out, very much. Perhaps they'd be a little happier if we just turned them loose and let them gallop away on their own, true. But every possible way I know how to assess a horse's enjoyment makes me believe that some horses enjoy being ridden.

I don't think it's being ridden that the horse enjoys, but rather doing the particular type of activity that they appreciate, which happens to involve a rider.

Halla appreciated going out with Nala, and she loved whatever it is she thought she was doing to Nala, communicating with or controlling her with body language and movements.

When I took Halla out and brought her down to get tacked up, she seemed very anticipatory. She was looking at Nala, and getting excited, and both Cammie and I could see she was pleased to be finally going out with Nala. It was the same as we rode down to the beach, with Halla taking on her usual leadership role with a little extra vigor.

On the beach, Halla was excited, but not extremely so. It was more like she remembered the drill, and she was ready and probably thinking we were going on a very long ride. When we turned around so soon (after less than a mile), the horses were fine with it. Nala had been ridden the day before, and Halla probably knew she was out of shape. It wasn't that she wanted to go home, but she was compliant either way. The only part where she got a little too hot was when we went up the last dune. I thought she shouldn't run because she had boots on, and I didn't want her to pull them off. She couldn't handle that, so took several massive leaps. The boots slipped a little, but they were fine enough to ride back home.

After the ride, Halla felt sound as a dollar so I decided to try next ride going barefoot, just leading her down to the soft grass and sand.

I told Cammie that I didn't trust Halla to show signs of being "off" in the heat of the moment, so decided to see how she seemed over the next few days, and if all remained well we could go a little farther the next week.

The next week came, and everything was fine. Nala's rider had her horse saddled before I arrived at the barn, so she went for a brief ride around the property. There was a fallen log in the tall scrub so she jumped it; Nala is a decent jumper.

Except apparently they had a bad takeoff so Cammie ended up off balance to one side, and said she didn't fall off but did a quick dismount. The stirrup banged her knee, and for a minute she thought, "I'm hurt," while realizing she was way back in the deep bushes where it could take awhile to be found. Of course, she had her cell phone on her. She told me all of this while laughing from atop her horse while she waited for me to finish saddling Halla.

At the beach, we did a lovely four mile ride. Some giant truck with huge tires was driving with a Border Collie chasing behind for a bit, and then went crashing into the shallow water. That made an unexpected sound, so Halla thought about leaving the beach for a couple seconds but then changed her mind. The truck stopped to gather the dog, spun a big cookie in the sand and left. I guess trying to keep a Border Collie's energy down can also be difficult.

Cammie said she kept going out with people and horses that had never been to the beach, and they were often half mad with fright and the owners even worse. She told them all that they would get used to it, and our horses were the proof of her theory as we cantered past burned out stumps and flapping plastic half buried in the sand with neither horse doing more than taking a glance at those things.

The temperature was in the sixties, but since Halla's hooves were cool and she showed no issues after the previous beach ride, we went farther and also I let her do some cantering. Didn't have a ton of choice, actually, because she was begging to get moving. Cammie assured me she saw no signs of her being "off" in stride, and I didn't feel anything abnormal, so let her do more.

We met a new horse on the beach, Cass. If I got the breeds right he was Friesian, Belgian and TB. We had our fifteen, sixteen, and seventeen hand horses out there together. Halla was quite uppity about making sure that Cass understood her status and assured him that Nala was her minion and he would soon be too.

His owner, Alice was laughing because if they followed Halla closely, he didn't dare pass her. I said, "You're saying, "go," and Halla is saying, "NO!"

CHAPTER TWENTY-SIX

Brave

On the next ride with Nala and Cass, dodging raindrops on a rainy day, Halla was marginally less unhappy about Cass' presence, but still flung her head around a lot. At one point, Cass came cantering up behind and his rider started laughing because as he neared Halla he began flinging his head too, like "guess we're all flinging our heads around now." From what I've observed, I think geldings are more prone to peer pressure than mares.

Nala and Halla preferred going side by side a lot of the time, while Cass lagged a bit. He could move out very well, but his default average speed was a lot slower than the two mares. Nala had the fastest average - left to her own devices she'd be zipping along for miles. Halla wanted to keep up badly, but on her own moved along a bit slower.

This was the farthest ride since laminitis, and Halla seemed to have no issues, and cool hooves afterward. The only thing I really noticed was that the sole thickness was improving slooowly, so we still had to avoid any kind of rocks.

At one point Nala took off in a gallop, and Halla was her usual self. As Nala left, Halla wanted to go too, began breathing fire (lightly), which I was very used to. I decided to manage it with a bit of controlled speed work through some deeper sand, so let her canter off. When her eyes flashed red a little and she tried to ramp into a real gallop, I focused on weaving her between some drift logs and other obstacles, so we ended up with controlled speed and she downshifted exactly where I asked her to slow.

Cass' rider came trotting up. I'd only glanced back to see that her horse seemed unconcerned and then stopped paying attention. I guess she hadn't seen us moving along before, and she was exclaiming about how she'd thought Halla's moves were going to throw me off a few times but she was amazed I'd ridden through. This made me laugh, because I'd grown so used to her antics that I only thought about managing them and remained unsurprised and undisturbed.

Although I know every horse has challenges, I decided it would not be an unwelcome thing for me to find as a next horse one that did not throw curve balls and fastballs constantly at the rider every single ride. It was like Halla and I were in a sword fight sometimes, parrying each other's moves. Yet it was not a battle/battle, but more of a video game battle - perhaps slightly more fun for the horse than the rider who got worn out at times.

We tried to go down a wooded trail, but the seventeen hand Cass didn't fit underneath or between the trees, so we had to turn back.

On the next ride, Cammie was busy so I rode a mile down the beach to meet up with Alice and Cass.

Halla went out quickly, and we trotted and cantered toward the beach access where Cass' rider parked her trailer. We didn't see any sign of a horse on the beach, so we started up the steep dune toward the parking lot, which excited Halla very much since we never went that way. She galloped up to the top, and then when we crested the ridge she saw that there were two horses and a trailer below. That certainly made her pause and size up the situation. Then she saw it was Cass, the horse she thought was a bit of a dumbo. So she put her nose in the air and we went down and stood waiting for the others.

There was a new, handsome fellow Halla had not met yet. Brave was seven years old, just getting started under saddle. He had just a few rides on him total, and had never been to the beach. Cass' rider had decided to bring him along and pony him off Cass.

Brave was a golden dun. He looked like a Kiger mustang but not quite, because he was a Kiger/Friesian/Arab cross. He was about Halla's height at 15.1 hands, and Halla thought he was very interesting, probably because he was only recently gelded so still had some of the stallion vibe going on.

Brave was very well behaved, but of course it was difficult having a brand new green horse ponying along, so we walked the entire ride - about six miles. Took quite awhile but it was a gorgeous evening and a great experience. Only two things got Brave to startle a bit. One was a little boy carrying a green shovel and swinging it around as he walked down the beach, and the other was the sight of two little Shih Tzu type dogs yapping and biting each other (they were on leashes). Everything else he took in stride.

Halla was very calm, and after we left the other horses we trotted and cantered on home but she was very accepting of the milder, slower type of exercise.

I believe I can learn to ride most horses (won't say all because I haven't tried them all), but some horses are very tricky and it takes a few rides or more to learn them and for them to learn you. Cammie and I traded horses the next ride, so I was on Nala and she was on Halla.

I wasn't going to try anything that might cause a potential problem. Cammie was a great rider, and managed Nala better than I did; they had worked out all the kinks in their relationship. Cammie seemed to wait for the horse to do something and then correct if necessary. This worked well for Nala, because she stayed mentally relaxed when she felt she could do what she needed to, i.e. trot off.

Unfortunately, if the person riding Halla used that method, Halla would also be quite happy but likely to go cantering off. Nala's rider offered that I could gallop Nala down the beach, but I knew that if I galloped Nala off, Halla was going to get very hot and start jumping around. If the rider didn't react to that immediately, Halla was going to take off and get strongly in control. I knew Nala wouldn't be held back if Halla came racing up because she was in the habit of being allowed to run for awhile in front. So my insecurities revolved around my horse not getting injured/injuring the rider, or even the ponied horse getting loose and racing me on Nala down the beach.

As it was, I asked if we could switch horses back near the end of the ride because Cammie allowed Halla to canter up and pass up several times, and I was worried if I let Nala run off, that Halla would end up going for a long canter or even gallop. I doubted I could slow Nala for at least a quarter mile, since her rider usually did not and she was bigger and stronger than I am. If she didn't get the knack of slowing Halla down, we might keep racing for longer, and Halla was not physically up for that.

So I consciously did what I knew I should not do, and when Halla raced by I held Nala back. The first time when she was frustrated, she leaped up and then planted one foot and spun a fast 360. Once we ended the circle, I let her out a little, we cantered, and the pause had been enough to let Cammie get Halla slowed so Nala was fine.

The second time Halla went by us, I decided to let Nala canter, but I restrained her stride and she was already stretching into gallop so she leaped high, half bucked and I wondered for a second if I had trapped her too much and she was going to begin bucking hard. I let out, reeled in, let out, and she calmed. But it was a real tight rope. So I asked Cammie if we could switch back, because we often let the horses move out the last mile, and I wondered how that was going to go if Halla kept passing us.

Nala's rider didn't want to trade, because we had swapped our stirrups out instead of moving them up and down a few holes, and they were very difficult to get back on the saddles.

So we continued as we were, but thankfully Halla was a little tired and kept to a slower pace so I long trotted Nala and let her stretch way out, which relaxed her.

When we got to our beach access, we saw that a giant elk herd was blocking the whole area, about fifty elk. There was no way around, so we tried slowly splitting the group by going through a narrow spot. As we came up the rise, an elk that was lying down stood up suddenly right in front of us and both horses spooked sideways about six feet. We passed through the group fairly easily, but once past there was this rushing sound and the whole herd started coming toward us. I felt vulnerable, so hopped off Nala and started saving my arms and yelling at the elk, which confused them so they stopped. Whew.

So no, I'm not a fearless rider at all, and was wanting to feel a bit safer than I did on that ride. Yet I did still enjoy it quite a lot. Nala was fun, had wonderful balance, a beautiful canter and jumped a log for me, which I couldn't do on Halla. Yet I had to think of the whole situation and try to control all the factors, which was pretty tough.

CHAPTER TWENTY-SEVEN

The Climb

In the landscape of our lives, our horses are not pebbles, they are mountains. What is a horse? An animal, a living creature; yet somehow, more.

Our time with a particular horse becomes deeply etched into the timeline of our life, and that horse is not a hobby like golf or fishing. We don't remember an experience or day as a fond memory of a good time; rather we have the Amore years, and the Valhalla years. Those years with a horse that changed us forever.

The days I spent with Halla on the mountain trails or the beach were not merely time spent with a good friend. Instead, she became we, a part of my identity, a piece of my soul that grew intertwined with my deepest self. She was the me that could express itself in the physicality of power and liberation. The me that sang out loud because of joy. The me that was profound quietness. Riding her was wind and waves, a clashing sound and overwhelming beauty.

With both my horses our relationships began in some anguish over the clash between a determination to give them a good life and to work with them versus the doubt I had in my ability to handle their exquisite and exhausting personalities.

I remember the heart pounding moments as I used every part of my wits and skill to keep Halla in check and wondering what was about to happen. I remember the feeling of adrenaline stabbing through the center of my chest. I remember the times she showed me that it was only the goodness of her heart that allowed me to control her, and that she clearly understood that at any moment she could take complete command of herself and do whatever she wanted.

I remember how it felt to move in perfect harmony, with her seemingly reading my thoughts and responding to them, rather than my cues. I remember her boundless pride in herself, and how she could swell up larger than the biggest horse I'd ever been on.

Somehow, and I don't know how or when, there was a turning point with both these horses where they went from teetering at the edge of too difficult, with two handfuls of reins overflowing, to an interesting puzzle, or a tricky game. The energy overflowing the dam began to turn the turbines. I learned them; their ways, their moves, what made them upset and made them calm. After studying the gauntlet, what seemed impossible turned out to be only patterns that needed to be understood.

With a new horse, I will begin the game again, learning new patterns. But I was not tired of the old ones yet. There was more to learn, would always be more. To learn a horse is like trying to memorize Pi or the sequences of DNA.

Mountains are treacherous, yet we dare to climb. They are sometimes synonymous with tragedy, with fear, with danger...but also with beauty, inspiration, and elevation of the soul.

You can't take a mountain out of the landscape. It will always be there, changing the shape of everything. You can't stay on the mountaintop forever. Soon there is another one to climb. Each is more beautiful than the last, but they cannot be compared to one another. Tragedy may await, but I keep climbing.

The first time I galloped on Halla, I thought I was going to be flung off into the bushes. Her muscles seemed to rotate around underneath me, almost like being on a merry-go-round in the wrong spot where you feel like you're going to get thrown off rather than held in by the centrifugal forces. But the forces did hold me on, and it was like sitting on a washing machine on top of a motorcycle. Mad-crazy-legs churning up the ground.

I would see her hooves coming up in front of us, and her whole body would feel like it was going to burst apart with the effort she gave. She loved galloping, and put her whole heart and soul into it.

All her life, in order to gallop all you had to do was think about galloping and you'd be doing it. To gallop was her default mode, her happy place. All the rest of the time spent riding was basically telling her it wasn't time to gallop yet.

A horse story is a love story. As with any love story, a horse story includes ups and downs, sickness and health, stormy days and sunny ones.

Yet how fortunate is anyone to be able to look back and remember that they had found such a relationship, so true, and deep, and meaningful.

CHAPTER TWENTY-EIGHT

Changes

Something was bothering me. Halla started to feel different when I rode her, not lame but not striding well. When the vet came out to check on her, we did an x-ray of her knees and saw that the catastrophic fall she'd had when younger had ended up causing some arthritis to her knees. Unfortunately, the knobbiest one with the most scar tissue also had a tendon that was calcifying, and it seemed to be causing some pain. The vet did some injections into the knee, and I decided to retire Halla to only light riding.

The injections seemed to help, and in the pasture she moved very well. However, she didn't quite feel like her normal self under saddle so I only took her on easy, slow rides around the fields.

Cammie went to go look at a Thoroughbred named Rascal. His owner had a rescue and saw Cammie riding Nala at a horse event, so had approached and asked her if she was looking for another Thoroughbred. Rascal had been returned to the rescue three times, and the owner really wanted him to find a permanent home this time. It was the opinion of the rescue owner that the failures had been because those who had tried adopting him had expected him to be less green than he was, and no one had spent the time needed to train him thoroughly. She thought he was calm enough to become a beginner horse with the right training. Cammie had a new boyfriend, and her hope was that if she and I got Rascal going, he might work out for her boyfriend to ride when she went out on Nala.

Since neither of my horses were able to go on serious rides anymore, I welcomed the chance to work with another horse. After bringing him to our barn, Cammie and I put several introductory rides on Rascal, lunged him and tried to figure him out a little bit. He did some interesting things at first like get stuck and seem unable to move forward, backed rapidly when nervous, and a lot of bucking on the lunge line. It seemed difficult for him to pick up a canter.

Cammie's boyfriend tried riding Rascal a few times. We didn't have a western saddle that fit him at first, so he went in a dressage saddle. Since Rascal was still very green, Cammie's boyfriend came off several times when Rascal hopped around or during failed mounting attempts. When I rode him, Rascal was a little spooky and reactive, but the most difficult thing he did was throw in a big buck or kick, especially when going down a hill or getting into deeper footing.

Cammie said, "Maybe if Rascal doesn't work out for my boyfriend, you would want him." I laughed at the idea, and told her firmly that I already had two horses, and even if one was retired and one mostly retired, they were definitely all I could afford. I knew how much I owed Amore, who had taught me volumes of things I'd never understood before about horses. Valhalla had been the best horse I'd ever ridden, and both horses were such good friends of mine. Even though I wanted to ride too, there was no way I would give them less time or attention than they deserved.

Also, Rascal was a very funky looking Thoroughbred. The word "Thoroughbred" can conjure up images of noble looking steeds, muscular and lean with long legs and balanced bodies. Horses like Nala. Rascal had a pointed hip, a mild version of what is called a "hunter's bump" caused by a steep hind end conformation and possibly some kind of injury of muscle strain. He had a "noodle neck" similar to what Amore had when I first bought her, a front pastern that turned out to one side, and as Alice said, "He looks like a committee put him together." Not all of his parts matched each other. I couldn't fathom him as a replacement ride for my super athlete, Halla or the lovely Amore.

Soon I took Rascal down to the beach with Nala, and it was very difficult to get him into the canter – he often did a huge leap or buck into it, so I tried to not interfere while keeping his head up a bit and waiting while he sorted out his body.

On the second ride to the beach, I almost got bucked off. Nala came around and Cammie was going to trot her next to us over a small log. Except Nala suddenly decided to come over it like she was dropping into a water jump. Rascal was still in "shadow" mode: when startled, he would mimic what the other horse was doing, just to be safe. So he immediately bucked into a leap with that same posture over nothing, while twisting to one side. His timing was so fast that they almost made the same move together, like dolphins leaping. As he was rising, I watched Nala's leap out of the corner of my eye. I caught him, but was slightly sideways so if he'd kept bucking I might have come off. Obviously, he thought Nala had seen something and was leaping out of the way and possibly galloping off.

Everything else went fairly well on that ride, a couple startles, a small spook. But I soon learned that Rascal's "go to" move was bucking. If the sand was too deep, and his hind end slipped a tiny bit, he'd throw in a buck. If he stepped on a piece of seaweed, buck. Going up the big dune off the beach, I'd keep him to a walk, but it was very deep after the storms now that it was November. The deep sand made Rascal insecure, so he would throw in bucks going up, sometimes quite big enough to pop me off the saddle and sometimes I would come down like we'd landed after a jump. He got a few reprimands, because all of these moves could have thrown off Cammie's boyfriend, who was supposed to be his primary rider. It might have been easier if he was allowed to go up the dune faster, but I knew if he learned to race up he'd probably try it with any beginner rider. It seemed like it would take some time to get this horse's mind working and relaxed.

It was time to worm the horses, something you wouldn't think would be entertaining, but it was.

First I sidled up to Halla, snaked my arm under her neck and around the top of her nose. By the time I brought the syringe to the side of her mouth, she knew what I was doing and looked at me reproachfully. I pushed the plunger and she froze.

"Poisoned."

She planned to stand there, not moving her tongue forever.

I left and went to worm Amore. Snuck up to her, slid my arm around her neck and around the top of her nose. She looked at me sweetly.

"Hi."

A moment later, she tried to move her nose toward her food. Immediately, she was hysterical.

"Can't reach my food! Can't reach my food!"

I pushed the plunger. Her eyes got soft.

"Oh. You were just putting food in my mouth. Good."

She tasted it. Her mouth opened and a wad of hay mixed with wormer plopped on the ground. I hadn't realized she had that much hay in there. I grabbed her nose and gave her the rest of the tube. She was starting toward her hay already and panicked again.

"Can't reach my food!"

I let go as her mouth opened and she grabbed a bite of hay, forgetting there was more wormer in her mouth. Chew, chew, swallow.

Looked back over at Halla, who was still standing frozen, not moving her tongue.

"Poisoned. I'll never move my tongue again."

I went over, opened Halla's mouth and moved her tongue around. Put a carrot in her mouth. It sat there. I moved her tongue and the carrot dropped out. Poison had ruined her tongue. I put a wad of hay in her mouth. It sat there, hanging out the side. She went and stood near her hay, looking at me forlornly, wishing she could eat, that she didn't have bitter poison in her mouth.

I scratched Halla and massaged her knees. One eye enjoyed the rubdown. The other looked disappointed that I had poisoned her. Finally I gave up and left, knowing Halla would eventually lose the bad taste and start eating the food I'd left for her. Amore rubbed her head on me while continuing to eat steadily.

While Halla was only going on easy rides, my friend Alice was trying to get her horse Brave some more riding experiences, so asked me if I would ride him on the beach sometimes when she went on her other horse, Cass. I ended up riding him on his second beach ride. We trailered a few miles to a different stretch of beach, and met up with some other women for a total of eight horses including Cammie and Nala.

I was a bit hyper aware on Brave, knowing things could go south quickly. There is a collection of things to consider that is different for each horse. In my mind on this ride was the fact that the group was large, and I didn't know most of the other riders. So I didn't know how Brave would respond to the other horses and if any of them might get out of control. Tempering that thought was the fact that the other riders were all in western saddles other than Nala's rider, and judging by their seats, the horses were not prone to doing unexpected things.

Alice let me ditch the running martingale she sometimes used, and we decided that I didn't need to be ponied. I used a double-jointed D snaffle since the O-ring we used last time had pinched Brave's lip on one side.

There is a difference between a hot horse, a green horse, and a hot, green horse. Brave was not hot. We were learning each other quickly, but I realized one reason I felt a bit tentative on him was that he was one of the few very green horses I'd been on that I didn't start myself. So I really had had no idea of what he knew other than that he'd been exposed to the environment we were riding in, and that he led well and cued off other horses.

As we rode, we figured a lot out. He was super smart, so we worked a lot on the fact that when my seat and legs were pointed straight, I wanted him to go straight, and I guided him back when he wandered. I tried hard to make each cue on and off with a quick release as soon as he responded. Without the martingale I had more feel, and found that he was not terribly claustrophobic. I could hold pressure for a couple seconds with him still using his brain and not panicking.

After Amore, I don't think of that as a given. Once upon a time she was a hot, green horse. It's a lot different being on a horse that you give a little pressure and he responds by thinking and moving, versus giving a tiny bit of pressure and flying all over the place, trying to figure out how to let the horse know which response was the one that you'd wanted.

The first time I asked Brave to trot he had no idea what I wanted. Not a clue. He'd not been asked to trot by the rider, only followed when the other horse trotted. I added a little leg pressure, gave rein, lifted my seat a little, and he got very tense and ready but tried walking faster. I told him to trot, and he walked faster still. Finally he tried a trot step and I loosened up everything and relaxed, telling him he was a good boy.

The second time I asked him to trot it only took him about five seconds, and the third time he picked it up right after I asked. He was very smart.

On the way back, Brave's owner asked everyone if they wanted to trot, and I said sure, so we all began trotting. Suddenly it felt very exciting and Brave's head was up and I asked him to slow a little and he trotted bigger. So I called ahead to his owner and asked her to slow down, which she did. We pulled off and let the others pass, and did a lurching circle. Brave so far either did these very huge irregular turns or he turned way too tight. Greenies.

We decided to trot again but put all the other horses in front instead of feeling like they were chasing us. Without the clopping hooves behind us, Brave settled nicely and relaxed into the trot on a loose rein, and slowed when I asked. My stirrups were way too long, but he was doing super well and I figured as long as he didn't buck real hard I'd be fine. He only lurched forward a couple times, we had gone in the water and his tail got wet, and I guess it scared him when it slapped against his leg. And once I saw a mosquito biting my arm and slapped it hard, which caused a startle. Oops, forgot I was on the greenie.

We went quite far away from the safety net of Cass, led and followed other horses, passed between groups and trotted all on our own. Brave did amazing. I relaxed as much as I could, and trusted him as much as I could.

He felt very different from many horses I'd ridden, and I don't know the Friesian temperament but he didn't quite feel like an Arab or a Mustang. His breeder wanted to create the perfect endurance horse, but I don't think she did. He felt like he would prefer to go slow.

He had very little spook or panic for a green horse, which was good. It was tricky to know how to manage his energy, because I was not used to this type of temperament. By the time he had a little panic, I was working up to take care of our "big problem," but by then it was over and I was left behind so to speak. "OK, here we....go." That would be the reactive type just getting their hooves underneath them in readiness for the bigger things to come. But with Brave it was already over.

One day I rode Cass while Alice rode Brave, and a motorcycle showed up on top of a beach dune suddenly. The unflappable Cass spooked pretty big, and Brave spun quickly enough to throw Alice off like a stone from a slingshot. She was bruised but not injured badly, but that was what she said Brave's temperament was like – he was not spooky but if he did go off it would be a big one.

Eventually, Alice didn't need my help as her horses were soon doing very well, and she could ride Brave and have her husband ride Cass. She was very good at ponying horses also, and Cammie and I would often meet up to take Nala and Rascal out for a ride with Alice, where she would be on Cass and taking Brave along on a lead line for the exercise.

CHAPTER TWENTY-NINE

Rascal

It's a lot to ask a horse to go out alone, when it's getting dark, when we can clearly hear the gates squeaking and the rattling of feed buckets as horses are being arranged into their night pens and fed dinner. I carried a crop, in case, and did have to swat Rascal once when he got frozen with ears swiveled back, listening to the other happy horses eating as we headed off into the unknown dusky fields.

He danced, a little, but it was nothing compared to Halla's complex ballet moves and he tired of it quickly. He had a rather soft mind and was not motivated to fight for what he wanted. He tripped hard once, over a dirt clod, and was emotional about it. I can't say what his emotion was, whether he got annoyed, scared, worried, etc but he disliked tripping. He did a flinging move, which lasted a brief half-second and I just said "You're fine," and he was back into work mode in a moment.

I know the secret to cantering unbalanced horses, or ones that feel like they will buck. So we found the hills and cantered up them. Horses have to get their heads down to buck, and this is very difficult uphill, especially if they're not super strong in the hind end. I gave Rascal loose reins, and worked on getting the feel of his canter, and trying to push him on when he wanted to stop.

He never made it more than a few strides, but on the third hill he put all his legs down in the right sequence, and balanced well with no hopping. We cantered up to a sharp corner where I needed to have him trot, and because of his good balance he had a very nice downward transition.

Good boy.

The next ride on Rascal was a very good one.

I lunged him first, which was mostly just to get some energy out because I was having him work just before feeding time again, alone. So he was a little worked up, not too bad but definitely making his opinions known. Mostly he just wanted to canter fast and squeal, but this was in the round pen and was the most balanced and least hoppy canter I'd seen him do yet, on a rather small circle. So I just watched him for a few rounds to help my psyche understand that he did have some good balance and was keeping all of his legs clear of each other while moving fast.

I'm not just cavalier about danger, since I've learned there are many ways horses can endanger themselves or their rider. I had some thoughts, wondering if Rascal kept hopping and bucking because he was unbalanced, or tripping now and then because of his offset pastern. Seeing him carrying himself well helped my logic, which gave me some confidence that Rascal could balance with a rider safely.

After hopping on, I rode him around the round pen several times, then out and around the fields. He did not want to go away from the barns, friends and food. I didn't let him stop to think about it. Away we went, and if he didn't go one way I'd turn him another way until he was confused. Then I sent him forward, always forward. If he tried going laterally, I'd send him forward faster.

He could pick up the canter very smoothly, if he got his legs right. It was starting to get better. The other very positive thing was that I sent him forward fast over very rough, uneven ground and he never tripped. He was starting to figure it out.

Something that helped was that I had changed him from a snaffle to a Kimberwicke bit. It seemed like he responded better to the slight leverage and was balancing himself better in it. The chain did not seem to bother him, which made me wonder if one of the other three people who returned him had tried a curb on him. Probably not at the racetrack.

Several times Rascal decided he was done with riding and wanted to go back to the barn for dinner. I was starting to get the feel of his "thing" he did when frustrated (bunching up and feeling explosive), and I didn't even circle him but just gave him a spank, hard legs and drove him on, not giving him time to stop and think, making him move off fast. That seemed to help his thinking for a while. My strategy was to reprimand, then move out. Hoping his brain worked best in motion, like many Thoroughbreds and Arabs.

I rode him faster than he wanted to go, which I enjoy doing to some horses. I'm not really about domination but it's a teaching point for the horse to understand he must try to work with the rider and not just do his own thing. Somehow if you ride them like the devil is on their back they start thinking: "Is she going to try to ride me right through that fence?" But it all works out and they realize you're rather assertive and perhaps even trustworthy - if you don't actually run into a fence and keep them safe.

If a horse presents himself strongly, and I decide it's not fear but just expressing opinions, then I want to introduce the idea that he may not understand just how powerful I am or what I can make him do.

Calling a horse's bluff is one thing, and perhaps he has gotten away with a "show of force" such as bucking and squealing. So although I know 100% that any horse can ditch me or dump me, I say to the horse, "You think you're getting me off? Think again!" And he starts to doubt his own power. Then I control his direction and speed, and soon hopefully we'll be having a conversation as a team, working together.

When I say I was riding him like the devil was on his back, I don't mean I was pushing Rascal with my legs but rather I just asked him to trot, and when he did, I gave him a loose rein, and when he started moving big, I posted that rhythm and kept looking ahead as if I wanted him to go as fast and far as he could. Meanwhile, his mind was thinking.

Then I rode him straight out to the end of the field, fast, and hopped off to let him graze. This surprised him, but he is a foodie and figured it out quickly. We wandered back toward the barn, stopping for nice patches of grass, until he seemed to wonder if he really did want to go home yet.

Back at the barn, we stopped along Badger the Quarter Horse's pen, and the two horses sniffed noses. Then Badger took Rascal's halter cheek piece and held it between his front teeth. Rascal stood there, and then tried to move away. Badger held him firmly by the halter. After another minute, Badger moved Rascal a couple feet down the fence line, using his halter. Nobody was getting hurt, and Rascal just obeyed Badger so I simply watched. Not sure if Badger was ever going to let Rascal go, eventually I flipped the end of the lead at Badger - he let go and we walked off.

CHAPTER THIRTY

Fright

On our next ride, I accidentally scared the pants off Rascal.

It was raining, but was my last day off work for a while so I was determined to get another ride in. Saddled up Rascal wondering how it would be trying to get him to go out alone to the beach in the rain.

Tried to make things pleasant, brought him into the main barn for saddling and let him wander around eating hay, bringing him back to stand for saddling and bridling. He seemed to enjoy this a lot more than standing at the saddle rack outside.

We made our way down to the beach, with me being very encouraging and asking him to trot if he felt like he was worried or about to get stuck. When we came over the last hill, we saw the path was covered with elk.

Unfortunately, there were about sixty of them, spread out over a good distance along the grass. It was going to be difficult getting enough space to go around.

At first I tried trotting forward, then we crept, and as we got very close a big bull with spiky horns lifted his head and Rascal froze. I started to feel his heart pounding against my leg - BOOM -BOOM - BOOM -BOOM.

For a few moments, I thought about staying on, then I realized after about twenty rides or so I didn't really know what might happen if Rascal got terrified, even though he was currently standing quietly. So I hopped off and led Rascal around the herd. He was very nervous and prancy, and blew a snort an Arab would be proud of, but eventually we got around the mob and carved our way down through the deepest dune to the beach.

Thankfully the elk stayed up top and didn't come down to play.

Rascal was a different type of horse; I guessed he would end up being less difficult than some. I walked him around in a very large circle, around and around, defining a big "arena" in the sand. Then we stood quietly, and he tried rubbing his nose on me, a habit I was trying to break. But definitely thinking about himself, his own comfort, and not about dying anymore.

I guess I try to be the Wizard of Oz for the horses I ride, granting them the chance to earn the gift of courage. Hopefully I work on building my own courage too.

So I got on, and did big circles and serpentines around the arena. There was a huge, very flat area today and we could stay on wet sand without getting into any loose stuff.

I thought about how poor Halla had never been able to make as nicely balanced circles as Rascal was already. When we'd started riding with Nala, we'd used the beach as an arena like this, and it had helped Nala tremendously but Halla just couldn't get balanced with her asymmetrical body and stayed somewhat crooked and rushed. I'd finally figured out her inability to go on a loose rein relaxed was because of that asymmetry, and even though Rascal was far from balanced, he was still far ahead of her and going around on loose reins, making nice circles just following the angle of my seat, legs, torso and shoulders.

Turning Rascal down the beach, the wind picked up a little but I thought I'd let him out to see if he'd canter. He wouldn't, because he wasn't quite secure enough to go that fast, preferring to keep a close eye on the drift logs and seaweed we were passing.

We turned back for home, and I hopped off to lead him back through the elk gauntlet.

They tried to bunch up and follow us a couple of times, but I made scary sounds and waved my arms until they thought twice about it.

Walking up the hill, Rascal led beside me like I'd wiped the floor with him. We went through the gate into our home field, and I thought, "Better quit while you're ahead." But then a line from a movie popped into my head, "You're not that far ahead."

So I circled Rascal around the field and asked him to give me a nice canter up the hill. I sat back and deep, and he gave me the sweetest rocking horse canter, well balanced and striding out. After telling him what a good boy he was, I turned him for the barn, and I can't tell you when I've ridden in such a quiet horse back to the barn. It was only a forty-five minute ride, but after thinking he'd be killed by the elk herd, and using his brain to follow all my directions on the beach, he didn't have a step of prance or jig or bobble left in him. He came in with a lowered head, extended walk, and didn't look at one thing until I stopped him at the barn door.

He got wads of hay, a nice brushing, and I told him he was going to be a working boy now. He chewed and thought and blew horse slobber on me.

Christmastime is very rainy in Oregon. When I arrived at the barn in the afternoon, all the horses were hunkered down in their sheds. Our sheds were tall, open, airy, clean and oriented in the right direction to block the worst weather. All the horses preferred to stand in them when the weather was bad.

When I was at home, I had wanted to ride. When I got to the barn, I really didn't want to. But I told myself, "Why would you even own waterproof riding pants if you weren't going to ride in the rain?"

The night before, I had been imagining how I was going to learn to really ride well in the next year. My visualizations were of my body perfectly balanced over my horse, moving in sync, my leg and rein cues smooth, distinct, releasing perfectly. Poetry.

In the real world, I got on Rascal and it was rainy, windy, cold and he wanted to be back hunkering down in his shelter. He dragged his feet, he pranced, he rushed, he stuttered sideways. In the real world, I kept him from running into the fence, from tumbling down a hill, from dashing home, from screaming "help!" to his buddies.

I think in the end he was just mouthing a silent ("help me").

My face was cold after one loop around the pastures, so I took Rascal down the hill and lunged him. The round pen was more sheltered, so we both felt better there. Rascal was starting to listen to my voice and do transitions when I asked 90% of the time. He didn't buck into the canter, and just worked so nicely. I was proud of him. He got lots of treats, and I believe he thought I was nuts but possibly didn't mean him any harm.

Nala had not been ridden in several weeks. She had a small toe crack that developed into some white line disease. Her rider tried soaking it and the farrier tried trimming it out, but it was continuing to move up so the vet came and helped resect the area. The farrier hot-set a shoe on, and left an open mouse-hole shaped area at the toe. They soaked it with Oxine to hopefully clean all the bad organisms out.

Of course, Nala is one that winds up after time off, so she was a bit wild.

Rascal, on the other hand was becoming confident. The first time Nala galloped into the air without going anywhere, Rascal thought about hopping around but let me stop him. After that, he just watched her and didn't react, no matter what she did. Nala could do several gallop strides in a row, with her legs doing four beats but with her rider holding her back so she didn't go anywhere except up and slightly forward. It was rather impressive. Made me wonder why they don't do a collected gallop in dressage competitions.

Obviously, Rascal had his own antics to try. He could have been called Shenanigans because he was full of them.

His audible expressions were varied and hilarious. He would squeal and sometimes snort like a pig. Not a soft kerfuffle or sharp blast, but an actual oink oink kind of sound. He also groaned loudly once in awhile, as if he was just being asked to do so much.

But we were making tremendous progress. He did spook a couple times, did a little hopping and tried rushing through a cue or two, and once I heard his right hind leg whip through the air behind my ear, even though his back didn't lift more than an inch or two. He must have had a quite flexible pelvis.

However, he was able to go around without tripping at all, and the sand was deep but he didn't buck. We cantered several times on the beach, and I never had to break him down for trying to rush off. There was no bucking or crow hopping, he just gave me a nice, round canter and kept it up once for almost a minute. We went safely down the steep dune onto the beach, which had built into quite a deep, shifty mountain due to high winds.

For the first time I felt comfortable to try riding up the dune on the way home, and Rascal walked, trotted and pulled himself right up without leaping or bucking.

It was starting to feel like I was with Rascal's movement now, and also that I "had his number." The trickiest part is when you're getting a horse going (or going again, with some horses) and the horse reacts, then the rider tends to overreact despite their best intentions. If you're not quite sure what is going to happen, the best strategy is to be sure you can handle it. But after a bit, you can read the horse better and know how far the spook is going to go, how fast the horse is going to calm down, and how bad their hops or bucks are. Then you relax more.

Having a comfort level with a horse means there are no overreactions or tenseness from the rider, and so the horse tends to relax more and more too. Within their mental capabilities, of course. I found myself going on a loose rein, most of the time. Hopping on a strange but trained horse, I never have this learning curve. With greenies and remedial or very hot types, I do.

I've been on many horses where I was told they were trained, used to the work, used to the environment and the feel from the horse was that this was true. When the owner said I could gallop the horse, I felt quite comfortable to do so. But I'm never going to hop on a Nala or a horse where they can't tell me what the background is, and attempt to gallop away without a good, long period of me getting to know the horse. Canter, perhaps, if all feels well.

After awhile on the beach, Rascal started putting his head down low and curling his neck under. I had been on a loose rein, so knew this was not an evasion. He also gave me no indication he was feeling like bucking. I suspected he was getting tired from using his hind end muscles. So I just let him do that for a while, and sure enough, after he rested for a bit he lifted his head and began working again.

CHAPTER THIRTY-ONE

Devastation

I'd been worried a bit for a couple weeks, noticing Halla had been looking a little more sore on her bad knee. We had several days of very nice weather, and someone told me they saw my horses looking happy, and Halla running around. I thought she might have done something bad to her knee, since she was limping one day. The next day she was worse, so I called the vet.

The vet asked if she could have laminitis again. I wasn't sure, but if it was I had no idea what more I could do since she was off grain and our hay was tested. Of course, it was January and the previous year in January was when she had foundered before.

When the vet came out, he said he had been seeing cases of laminitis even though it was January, and soon diagnosed Halla with laminitis again. There had been a warm spell with temperatures in the sixties the previous week, so it was not "winter laminitis," but "spring laminitis" in January.

I had been so comfortable having Halla on grass even after the laminitis, because she tested negative for Insulin Resistance and Cushing's. The vet said the science wasn't yet that perfect, and there was a spectrum where the horse might not yet test positive but keep getting laminitis, and then later would test positive. I remembered hearing that some horses with really bad numbers would for some reason sometimes do better than others that were barely positive for Cushing's or Insulin Resistance. We sent off bloodworm to test her again.

My hope was that this would turn out to be a far milder case than the previous year, because I had caught it so early. This year she only reacted mildly to the hoof testers. I put her in special padded boots, and into a sand paddock where she could be close to the pasture where Amore and Nala were turned out, and they could visit over the fence.

The vet noted that he saw some abnormal fat deposits on Halla, even though she was thin, which could be a sign of Insulin Resistance. It didn't seem to be the worst-case scenario so far, and I was very hopeful that Halla would have a good recovery again, and be sound enough to play in the pasture with her friends.

Over the next several weeks, Halla's pain seemed to get worse instead of better. She became so painful that she had not been able to walk out of her sand pen, and mostly stayed in one spot or lay down to rest. I started icing her hooves, and kept the Cloud therapy boots on at all times. Meanwhile, she remained on high doses of anti-inflammatory medications. She still ate her hay, and her eyes were bright and interested in her environment. However, she would shift her weight between her feet when standing to help relieve the pain, and I could see trenches in the sand where she had sometimes struggled to get up after laying down. At night I struggled with nightmares, or did not sleep, anxious over knowing what was the best thing to do for my poor horse.

The tests came back and she was positive for Cushing's and also Insulin Resistance. The vet said it would take weeks for any treatment to help with either of those things, and all we could do was wait and see how her founder would end up. Her x-rays were very bad, showing that her coffin bones had rotated more than the previous year, and her soles were very thin.

My time and attention was mostly taken up with the intensive care Halla needed; giving medications, icing her hooves, trying to improve the angles, adding padding and boots to see what might make her feel better. Occasionally I would take Rascal out for a ride, or take Rascal and Amore out together for a walk to try to distract myself and cheer up a little.

For a couple of weeks it was a roller coaster ride of emotions. One day Halla would appear bright and cheerful, and I would be convinced she would improve and make it through. Then I'd be at home and someone would text me from the barn saying Halla was laying down under her feeder, looking miserable. I'd prepare myself for the worst, and plan to call the vet to have my mare put down when I got to the barn to check on her. But when I'd show up, she'd be up nickering at me and seem happy to be brushed and eat her hay. It wasn't long before I realized this was nothing Halla would be able to come back from and have a good life, especially when I studied the x-rays and saw how much damage had been done inside her hooves, and also when I realized she was only tolerating standing because she was on the maximum dose I could give her of pain medications. The pain was not diminishing after several weeks, and we were approaching a month after I'd noticed the initial lameness.

One day things took a turn. I'd been watching for abscessing, knowing it can be very common after founder. I noticed her soles were starting to get deep grooves of separation around the edges, and her worst hoof started peeling up around the sides; the sole was starting to loosen and come off. I knew if that came off, the small amount of protection over the coffin bone would be gone. I looked at pictures of exposed coffin bones online, and my husband and I decided we would not risk that happening to her.

So we made the appointment to have Halla put down.

When the day came, it was beautiful and sunny, my day off work, the vet was still available, and so was the man who runs the tractor at the farm.

My husband and I went out several hours early to spend time with Halla. She had a very good day. With some extra Bute, she was eager to get out of her pen for the first time since her laminitis and walk around eating grass. We gave her apples and carrots, and brushed her the way she'd always loved, and the sunshine made her coat look glossy and bright.

People from the barn wandered through, there was a new puppy to cheer us up, hugs all around and stories told. One of the horse owners had just put down her very old dog that afternoon, so that was a very long hug. Tears flowed.

On the other hand, we could see how different Halla was. She enjoyed herself very much, but when we turned her loose after being pent up for weeks she did not even try to trot, just walked slowly. Even with her horrible knee injuries and previous founder episode she had almost always tried to trot to see if she could. Also she did not roll, or pay much attention to Amore or Nala, but grazed on her own, which she would never have done normally.

So I believe she knew that her place in the herd was changing and perhaps horses detach knowing the herd would naturally move on without them if they couldn't keep up. We also knew that the damage she was doing with the grass, treats and movement would make her pain much worse on the morrow, if we somehow changed our minds.

We hugged Halla and she leaned on us and enjoyed the attention. When it came time to walk over to where the vet would be, she did not want to go. It wasn't that she understood anything that was going on, but rather she thought we were going to put her back into her little pen. Which confirmed to me that she would never have been happy living like that long term, even if we could have stabilized her hooves somehow. After this she could have never been turned out on pasture again.

The vet sedated her and then gave the euthanasia, and she went down easy. We helped move her a few feet into the side of the hill and watched her buried. Rebel's owner brought daffodils, which we put on top of the hill. She was laid next to Dexter and Simba, two old horses we'd seen pass since I began boarding at the farm, and the flowers were blooming over Simba's grave where his owner planted them a couple years before.

Before the burial, we brought Nala and Amore over to see Halla's body and sniff her, and then they both moved on with their lives as horses often do. The vet said horses deal well with death, but not with a horse going suddenly missing, so she recommended that we show them that Halla was dead so they didn't get upset and look for her that night. They went in their pens and began eating as if it had helped them to understand.

We continued to cry and grieve, of course, but there were other animals that needed us – Amore, plus our cats, birds and dog at home. I suppose I could have felt bitter about losing my horse too soon. But I understand how blessed I was to have owned such a wonderful horse for nine years. Every day was a priceless gift.

In the days that followed, family and friends showered kind words on me. One quote I thought was especially helpful was "A good death is never a given, even for a good life. Some are lucky both ways." Thankfully, I was able to make the decision to help Halla out of her suffering, and make it up to horse heaven where friends like Cheyenne, her favorite lead mare and Beau were waiting. Somewhere she could eat all the grass she wanted and gallop faster than any other horse, I am sure. Probably up there her snorts and hooves were actually flames and she could roll and never get dirty.

How odd it was that so many times I felt as though Halla was just short of being too much for me, but yet she had always stayed just below that threshold. So many times I thought, "If she gets any hotter or more explosive, I am going to fly off." But somehow she would stay in that moment just barely manageable, and so we had continued on our way.

For the last few years, it was strange how I could take her out with a beginner on an easy trail ride, and I would know that we could still manage the ride and keep that person safe on their horse. Many experiences with Halla taught me that when she needed to be manageable, she would be. And when she didn't need to be manageable, she would be just manageable enough.

Of course, there were those rare times when something unexpected would happen, and we'd lose it. But it was a very rare thing for me to come off Valhalla, even when she was as green as grass. She never was trying to get me off. Coming off her was due to something spooking her violently, or tripping her. She never was scooting out from under me or dropping a shoulder or twisting away from my seat (aka Amore).

So many things made Halla the most fun horse to ride. When I only had Amore, if someone wanted to ride my horse so I could ride another bigger, faster horse, I was always happy about that. After I had Halla, my own horse was always my first pick, because she was the most fun to ride – the most fun horse I've ever ridden.

CHAPTER THIRTY-TWO

The Hero Saves The Day

In the weeks after Halla passed away, my husband and I were preparing to go on a vacation to Japan. It made me feel better to have several rides on Rascal, and to take Amore and Rascal out for walks to explore and graze together. I noticed that Rascal and Amore got along very well together, and would happily graze side by side. Rascal was about 15.3 hands tall and made Amore look like a little pony next to him. My thoughts began to drift toward what kind of horse I would end up with now that Halla was gone. I contacted an Arabian rescue and discussed coming to see some of their available horses after I came back from our vacation.

Although I looked at horses for sale and pictures of many extremely beautiful and athletic examples of various breeds, my mind kept coming back to one thing. It turned out, I was more than a little fond of Rascal. Despite his shortcomings in physical aptitude and attractiveness, he was another horse that was not finding his place in life due to being misplaced and misunderstood. I'd been trimming his hooves for a few months now, and his crooked leg was not as off-kilter as it had seemed at first. He was developing some muscling over his hunter's bump, and it did not look as pointy. Plus his noodle neck was filling in a bit. Perhaps these things were true, or perhaps I was looking at him with different lenses over my eyes, ones that filtered everything through the bias of affection.

Before leaving on our vacation, I emailed Cammie and told her that if she didn't think Rascal was going to be a good fit for her boyfriend (something fairly obvious), that I would be willing to give him a home. He had been a free horse from the rescue, and it seemed possible that Cammie would give Rascal to me as well, if her boyfriend was not too attached. He did spend time with Rascal when at the barn, and thought he had a funny personality.

While we traveled for a month, in between enjoying the wonders of a foreign and fascinating country, I often thought about Rascal and grew very attached to the idea of having him as my horse. It seemed more and more like something that was perhaps meant to be; he'd showed up at the barn needing training right when Halla had needed to cut back on riding because of her arthritic knees. Although I enjoyed riding almost every horse I ever sat on, I was able to ride other horses at the barn without getting so attached. Because of Rascal's silly antics and personality, along with the challenges he presented to a rider, he appealed to me. If he'd settled right down with vigorous riding, and seemed appropriate for Cammie's boyfriend, I would never have thought of Rascal for myself. But after the time I'd spent working with him, we'd become friends, and he was a friend of Amore also.

It bothered me a little that Rascal seemed a bit limited in athletic potential, and even though young, he did not seem to be a candidate for jumping or endurance. Then it occurred to me that Amore was twenty-seven, and even if Rascal did not enjoy or have the aptitude for some types of riding I might wish to do, perhaps in a few years after Amore passed away, I'd have another more athletic horse that would complement Rascal nicely.

When we arrived back from our vacation, I headed to the barn to check on Amore. The barn owner spotted me right away, and said, "I hear Cammie's boyfriend is hoping you will take Rascal." My heart leaped at her words, and I realized how disappointed I would have been if they had turned down my offer. I contacted Cammie as soon as I got home, and we finalized the deal – she had been the official owner of Rascal and now she passed over his ownership to me.

It felt like it was meant to be, right away. There was only one problem, which was that I didn't think of Rascal as a rascal. He was mischievous, so in that way his name fit. But I didn't want to think of him as some sort of naughty character, always trying to get things to go his way. He was really a good boy, and needed something to live up to in his new life, that stretched out ahead of us. He had just turned ten years old, after all, and was younger than either Amore or Halla when I'd ended up with them.

So I renamed Rascal, and a Hero was born.

Hero had been off work for a month while I was on vacation, so I brought him back into fitness slowly. I'd never worked him very hard, previously, because I'd always kept in the back of my mind that he was meant for a novice rider, one that needed to stay in control and not have a hot horse rushing off with him. Now there was a freedom to really work Hero, and allow him to match what he did with his body to his mind.

There was a lot of bucking and kicking as we went along, and it puzzled me that as he got more trained and more fit that he still used so much energy to do it. Slowly I began to notice a pattern, and realized I could predict perfectly when Hero was going to kick out, buck or get upset. It was always when going down a hill, and steep hills seemed to really flummox him. He also struggled in deep footing, such as dry sand. Something else he'd always done was drag his hind hooves at times, and with all the extra work he was beginning to wear down the fronts of his hind toes significantly.

Reading on the internet, it wasn't long before I discovered what was going on with Hero. His behavior matched the symptoms of locking stifles, and once I knew what was going on I could see the stifles popping with certain movements, and feel it happening under my hand. As advised, I tried getting him even more fit, which helped a little but not completely. When I had the vet come out, she gave him some pain medication which he took for a month while I worked on strengthening and stretching his quad muscles that assisted with proper stifle function.

This made a tremendous difference, and soon Hero was picking up his canter smoothly, cantering through deep sand without bucking, and going down hills without bucking. The poor horse had been dealing with this painful condition for a long time, and the effects of this were a big part of what had made him difficult to ride and progress with training under previous riders. Some horses have stifles that lock the leg up completely so they can't move forward, and this is easy to spot. Since his condition was difficult to notice, all of his issues seemed purely behavioral.

It seemed like he might always buck on occasion, so perhaps he would not ever be suitable for an inexperienced rider. After so long with locking stifles, he'd figured out that kicking back or bucking would unlock his stifle and allow him to continue forward. Being an athletic Thoroughbred, he'd pull these tricks out midstride. Because this had helped him so well in the past, if Hero ever felt insecure or lost his footing a bit, he'd anticipate that throwing in a buck might help, and would do so with vigor.

Like Halla, Hero was not antagonistic toward his rider and only doing what helped himself out. Although on occasion I'd get tossed forward a bit from a big buck, he was not trying to unseat the rider, would generally continue along the line of travel, and it was not only within my current level of riding, I soon got quite used to it. After Amore, I'd not realized it was possible to become somewhat lackadaisical about bucking, but with Hero it soon became the norm.

Even after a year of riding, he still did not have the strength to hold a gallop for more than a stride, with the recovering hindquarter strength, but could lengthen his stride far more than previously. His speed was nowhere near Nala's, and not even matching Halla's, but he was still an enjoyable horse to ride. He had a wonderful long trot that could match Nala's slow canter, and although his canter was not fast, it was lofty, round and powerful.

By now, Hero had some stories of his own, and the beginnings of an intriguing life also. Any reservations I'd initially had about physical limitations he might have were quickly overcome as we became friends, and as I began to discover all of the delightful nuances of his unique personality. After all, a friend cannot be valued for what they can do, but rather must be appreciated for who they are. As his new book began to be written, the future pages of life unfolded before us, blank and waiting for the adventures we would have.

Amore's story was still being written, although we were certainly most of the way through her book. Valhalla's story was over, but not truly, because horses like her live forever in our memories, and in our hearts. Horses can live for more than thirty years, but I've not been able to have one in my life for even twenty yet, due to ending up with older horses. Yet it's not really about the length of time horses spend with us, but about their ability to etch their stories deeply into our lives, our thoughts, and our memories.

Halla was like a fire that burned all the time. She burned with energy, burned into my soul. There were painful things about knowing her, such as the way she'd suffered before I met her, and the way she suffered from the injuries and illnesses that plagued her life. Yet these things barely damped down her fire, and she spent most of the life she shared with me burning brightly and filling my life with a light I'd never known.

A fire like that cannot go out completely. It doesn't leave behind ashes, or darkness, but instead sends a light forward into the future, one that can be followed and cherished throughout the rest of life.

Evelyn May has been riding and working with difficult horses in the Pacific Northwest for the past twenty years. In addition to horse biographies, she writes about horse training and has a series of expanded fairy tales. She is an avid runner and enjoys exploring the deep woods and beaches along the coast.

Made in the USA
Las Vegas, NV
06 February 2022

43225171R00096